Emotional Intelligence:

The Complete Guide to Improving Thoughts, Behavior, Relationships and Social Skills

(The EQ Book)

D1566430

Table of Contents

Chapter 7 – Identifying Impacts on Emotions   65

Chapter 8 – Reading Body Language by Emotion   74

Chapter 9 – Body Language According to Personal Distance 85

Chapter 10 – Reading Body Language 93

Chapter 11 – Reading Body Language by Haptics 100

Chapter 12 – Surface Message vs. Deeper Message
103

Chapter 13 – Managing Self-Awareness   106

Disclaimer

The contents of this book are designed to help people understand what they can do to improve their emotional intelligence. It is essential that anyone who follows this book is cautious with the information offered.

The details listed here are based on many findings regarding how emotional intelligence works. The information should be used as a guide, but it is also essential to consider one's own judgment when trying to build one's EQ.

The publisher of this book cannot be held responsible for any difficulties or problems that come about when using the contents of this book incorrectly. Readers are encouraged to be ethical and considerate when building their EQ totals while also being observant as to how they are influencing others.

Introduction

The brain is the most active part of the human body. The brain is always changing with many emotions being incited each day. There are no limits to how many emotions a person might feel in a typical day.

People can go from feeling positive at the start of the day to negative at the end. A person might develop worries or preoccupations during the day. Maybe there are certain events or instances in one's routine that might trigger certain emotions. Everyone is different, but it is through the brain that life can quickly change. People have to know how their brains are working if they want to move forward and feel stronger about themselves in the future.

It is fascinating to see how people have many emotions that change throughout the day. However, for some people, those emotions can cloud their judgment. They might not think clearly and handle situations poorly.

Sometimes a person will feel too many emotions at once and the emotions might cause mental fatigue. There is also the chance that a person might try to read the emotions of other people but will struggle in doing so, thus leading to some awkward and potentially hostile moments.

People must understand what they are feeling while having plans for managing their emotions in the smartest way possible. The challenges involved in keeping emotions under control can be frustrating, but they are points that have to be reviewed appropriately. It is even more important for people to know how they can develop their emotions and make them work to their advantage in the workplace.

It takes a great deal of effort for someone to build the skills needed in the workplace to complete various tasks and to be more productive. Even the most talented and knowledgeable person in the world will not be capable of handling certain tasks if they do not have the emotional intelligence needed to handle certain situations in life.

Those who have a high emotional intelligence will understand and recognize the needs that people have in a workplace. This includes knowing how to identify what people are feeling and the attitudes that they hold in any situation. By working with a good emotional intelligence, it becomes easier for a person to thrive and succeed. The best part is that emotional intelligence can develop over time to provide a person with an improved standard of living.

This guide offers information on what people can do to acquire the skills they need to be capable of handling their emotions and getting the most out of their work. The information in this guide includes details on what can be done to manage different emotions and how to keep them from being problematic.

People can use many points for handling their emotions. This includes being aware of the emotions they have and how much effort they are putting into regulating those feelings.

The points in this guide are vital to success in the workplace. It is through one's emotional intelligence that a person can go far and succeed in a work environment. In fact, the points in this guide could work for people in any environment including at home and in personal relationships with other people.

The amazing thing about emotional intelligence is that it is an aspect of life that can dictate many things that happen.

When a person expresses one's emotional intelligence, it becomes easier for them to move forward in life and get the most out of any situation.

Chapter 1 – What Is Emotional Intelligence?

The emotions that people carry with them throughout the day are diverse. People can go from feeling happy to sad to excited to worried. Sometimes a person could experience all of these feelings in just a few hours.

These emotions are vital to everyone's life. The emotions that people have will dictate many of the things that they do. The things that people think and feel are always more powerful than the actions they do. It is vital for a person's emotional intelligence to be managed well. However, it is important for people who want to improve their EQ to understand what it entails and how it can be used.

The first thing to do when working with emotional intelligence is to understand what it is. Emotional intelligence is a vital part of life that all people need to possess if they are to be successful and strong-willed individuals.

Emotional intelligence refers to a person's ability to manage one's emotions and to handle the emotions of other people as well. It is about knowing what someone is feeling and having the ability to identify what makes those feel different. A universal sense of control is needed for making this part of one's life easy without adding anything frustrating to the relationship.

This concept is also known as the EQ or emotional quotient. It is different from the traditional intelligence quotient that is utilized to measure a person's intelligence.

Emotional intelligence has been a topic of interest to many businesses and organizations over the years. Although the concept of EQ was first introduced in the 1960s, it was not until the later part of the twentieth century that people began to take note of EQ. This happened because mental health and a person's ability to perform on the job have become very important considerations.

The Five Main Categories

There are five categories of emotional intelligence. The five points were introduced by Daniel Goleman, a prominent behavioral sciences expert. Goleman released these five-steps based on understanding what people can do to be stronger leaders in the workplace and to be more proficient in what they can do when helping others. The concepts continue to be important to this day:

1. Self-Awareness

This refers to how well a person is aware of emotions in one's self and other people. This includes having a clear idea of what people might feel when handling emotions and seeing what causes them to develop.

2. Self-Regulation

Self-regulation is the act of having control over one's emotions. This includes knowing how long an emotion will last and what can be done to keep an emotion from persisting.

3. Motivation

Motivation is how to use goals and efforts in one's life. This includes seeing what a person can do while using the right emotions to get where one wants to go.

4. Empathy

While emotional intelligence often focuses on knowing one's own emotions, empathy is knowing how others feel. This includes understanding what people are thinking and knowing how to react.

5. Social Skills

The ability to interact with people in a positive fashion is vital to one's success. A person with a high EQ will have the social skills needed to get along with others. This includes understanding how to manage nonverbal communications.

These five points will be discussed in their individual chapters throughout this guide.

EQ May Be More Important Than IQ

A good intelligence quotient or IQ is helpful for life. Knowing and understanding how to make logical and rational decisions is advantageous to everyone. At the same time, that IQ can only take people so far.

For instance, Jeffrey, a business executive has a very high IQ. He has thought of with many useful ideas for his business, and yet he is unable to get his business to expand or grow. He is having a hard time maintaining his payroll because people are constantly leaving the business.

Why is Jeffrey unable to get his business to grow? He is struggling with his EQ. He is not fully appreciative of his employees. Perhaps he does not understand that they need some balance between their work and their personal lives. This includes issues where workers are not satisfied with their jobs or are feeling too tired or uncomfortable with their work. But Jeffrey does not have the empathy to understand this.

As a result, it becomes hard for even his smartest ideas to thrive and grow. If he had a better EQ, he would make more plans based on what other people need. By adapting his ideas and values around what others want, it would become easier for his business to grow and thrive.

It is through one's EQ that it becomes easier to evolve and change.

What Makes It Different from Personality?

What makes EQ different from a person's standard personality? EQ focuses more on feelings while the personality is all about a person's style.

There are three things that make up every person:

1. The intelligence quotient

2. The emotional intelligence

3. General personality

Personality is hard-wired into one's brain. It is how a person would interact with others and behave in some fashion. Someone's personality can never change.

The EQ is different as a person can develop it over time. When a person is trained well, it becomes easier for that person to be active and positive. Many points about improving one's EQ will be covered throughout this guide to provide simple ideas for what they can do to get their lives to move forward.

A person's IQ is likely to stay the same throughout one's life. A person has a certain ability to learn things at a specific rate. It might be easier for a person to learn emotions and how to manage them if that person's IQ is not low.

EQ might be related to IQ when all is considered. When a person's EQ is high, it becomes easier for someone to want to learn. That person will use one's IQ to one's advantage. The emotions become balanced so that people fully understand what they can do to grow their lives. As a result, a person will use one's intelligence at a slightly better rate.

The emotional intelligence that a person holds is important for all people who want to accomplish the most in their workplaces.

Chapter 2 – What Makes EQ Special?

Emotional intelligence is more than just something relating to knowing what people feel. It is to understand and recognize what can be done to help others or to at least get along with them.

It is through a person's EQ that someone can get the most out of life. Anyone who has a high level of emotional intelligence will be more likely to succeed and thrive in one's work. There are several positives of one's EQ that must be explored. These points are vital for the workplace in particular as they relate to what people can do to move forward and thrive in their jobs.

Get Along With People

A workplace is often a challenging place. Each person brings their personalities, their biases, and their different levels of intelligence and experience to the work environment. They have to work in harmony and this is not always easy. There is also the added pressure of competition involved. Personal relationships outside of the workplace can be difficult at times as well. People often struggle with maintaining friendships. Finding a long-lasting romantic relationship can be challenging to some people.

Those with a high EQ are better equipped to get along with others. A high EQ individual will understand the ups and downs of relationships and make smart plans to avoid conflicts and to settle disagreements effectively.

Become More Productive

People who have a high EQ are more likely to be productive. Those people understand what they want out of their lives and aren't afraid of putting in the effort.

Let's say that there were two software engineers, Janet and Tom. They are working on the same task. Tom does not have much EQ and is not fully aware of what he wants to get out of his work. Janet is on the opposite end in that her EQ is high. Janet feels motivated in her work because she has her emotions in check. She knows how to identify what her co-workers are feeling and is capable of keeping negative emotions from persisting. She can produce her work easily. Tom is different as he is often worried about what will happen and is trapped in a mindset of uncertainty.

Janet will do more with her software engineering task because she is comfortable with herself. Her high EQ ensures she will find solutions for concerns she has about the work she is doing. All the added productivity allows someone to have more control over various functions and actions surrounding what one is doing in life. This, in turn, helps that person to feel emotionally positive about life. It becomes easier for many tasks to be done as one's emotions are kept in control.

People who are not emotionally intelligent will have a difficult time managing their thoughts, and this will keep them from being productive. A person might become overly worried when a new task is introduced and it is different from what one might be used to. A person with a low EQ might be afraid of what will happen if a project does not go right. All that worry and fear will cause a person to not do well with a task, thus falling into the trap of not knowing what to do to fix a problem or make things work right.

Stay Accountable

People often shift their responsibilities and try to keep things from being too complicated. They don't want to do things because they resist doing it, or maybe they are not aware of what to do to fix the problems that happen. Others might not be aware of the circumstances surrounding what they are doing.

Accountability is a necessity for people in any workplace. A person who is accountable for one's actions and work is not afraid to accept responsibility for their actions. It is through accountability that a person is capable of showing maturity and is able to recognize the duties and functions one has to enter into every day. This includes not only what is done correctly but also any errors that might occur. A person with a strong EQ will be more likely to stay accountable.

Accountability provides a person with the ability to take control of a situation. That person will understand that he or she is doing something valuable or necessary. By working with the right plans, it becomes easy for a person to stay accountable and confident with what one is going to do with life.

Easier to Manage Risks

There are risks to everything in life. A person might get into a car and go driving to the grocery store, but that someone is getting into the risk that the car will malfunction or someone might cause an accident on the road. Meanwhile, a person who plays gridiron football might enjoy playing it, but that individual has the risk of suffering a substantial injury like a concussion.

There are risks involved in every aspect of every workplace. One of the greatest reasons why errors are often made in the workplace is because workers are not fully aware of the risks and what they can do to lessen them. This can cause people to panic when something happens they did not anticipate. They might not have the emotional fortitude to handle some of the events that occur. Those who can handle and figure out their emotions will have an easier time moving forward and keeping everything under control.

A person's emotional intelligence can be utilized to figure out what one's abilities are and how well certain tasks may be completed. Knowing what can be done to fix issues and having a plan for emergencies is essential.

Avoid Questions

When a person has a low emotional intelligence, they are not certain about the decisions they made. They lack self-confidence. One of the most common questions that a person might ask is what he or she was thinking about in the past? For instance, a man who made a difficult move in the past might ask himself, "What was I thinking? I can't believe I did something that way. Why did I do that?" That man would have failed to use his emotional intelligence. People make rash decisions when they are not thinking about the results or consequences. They might think about the results that they want to attain, but they never think about why they want it or what they can do to maintain those results.

Emotional intelligence is needed to help people to have faith in what they are deciding to do. People need emotional intelligence to stay comfortable and focused on whatever it is they want to work on. More importantly, there will be less confusion when a person's EQ is strong. That person will not question their own decisions. People with a high EQ will not likely ask questions of other people in the workplace or in other situations. A person who asks lots of questions is revealing their low self-esteem and low self-confidence.

A Matter of Trust

People are loyal to people that they trust. One person might seem to be more intelligent than another, but what if that smarter person is difficult for people to trust? That intelligent person might be seen as stubborn or difficult to work with. An intelligent person might not have the emotional intelligence needed to deal with people. When EQ is missing, that person is not capable of understanding or having empathy toward others. But when a person has a high emotional intelligence, that person becomes easier to trust. This leads to added success and control over any situation.

It is through a trust that people can stay positive around others. When people trust each other, they are willing to support one another through anything that might come about in the workplace. Trust focuses on people showing that they recognize each other's emotions and are willing to support each other. People who trust one another are likely to get along and feel better in each other's company.

Without trust, it becomes hard for a business to grow and thrive. More importantly, a personal or romantic relationship will not get off the ground if the people involved do not trust each other.

Managing Customers

An interesting part of working with EQ is that it concentrates on how well people are able to interact with each other in a workplace. This includes working with customers in a smart manner.

It is easier for businesses to grow when its employees have EQ. An employee needs a high EQ to have a sense of empathy with customers. When a person understands the emotions of others it becomes easier for that someone to market a product. Having an understanding of emotions is vital for success. This is especially true of the workplace when customers are involved. Every customer should be treated with respect and care to ensure there are no problems that can't be dealt with.

Let's say that Sally is working to sell a car. She might notice that a customer is nervous about the process of buying a car. She can empathize with the customer and talk with that person about the process. Sally might explain what makes a car an attractive investment. She may also identify questions that people have and provide smart answers to those issues. By using her EQ, Sally is getting in touch with the customer and is showing that she cares about that customer's needs. This will make it easier for her to sell the car to that customer.

It is through the EQs of its employees that relationships with customers can be built. When the employees are capable of working with customers well, it becomes easier for people to feel comfortable with each other while doing business.

A Vital Foundation for Other Skills

The emotional intelligence that one has is the foundation of many skills. A person who has a high EQ will have many great skills:

- Time management – A person will know how to handle one's time and budget certain times of the day for specific tasks.

- Decision-making – People with high EQ can make the smartest possible decisions.

- Communication – It is a necessity for a person to communicate with others. A high EQ is often associated with strong communication skills.

- Stress tolerance – Those who do not have a high EQ will break down under stress. A person might not have an ability to manage certain ideas or actions because that person is incapable of handling the associated stress.

- Anger management – People who do not have control over their emotions are more likely to become angry because they don't know what to do. When someone has a high EQ, those emotions are easier to manage and allow a person control over situations.

- Presentation – It will be easier to use one's presentation skills to one's advantage if the person has a high EQ. The presentation is closely associated with the ability to communicate effectively.

By having a high EQ, a person has an ability to handle many things in one's life without struggling.

Chapter 3 – The Key Abilities of Emotional Intelligence

People who improve their emotional intelligence will find that there are many worthwhile benefits.

Be Ready to Review Oneself

Emotional intelligence is all about taking a look at one's life and identify one's feelings and thoughts. When a person can handle this, it becomes easier for that person to grow. The self-assessment process allows a person to look back at what one has done in life and to find solutions for handling any problems or issues that might have happened. It is through retrospection and identifying what is happening at the moment that a person can figure out where one's life is going and what can be done to keep everything under control. This is not always the easiest thing for a person to do, but it is vital to one's success in life.

Being Ready to Adapt

It is often a challenge for people to make it through certain situations in their lives. Whether it is trying to complete a test in school or talk with an employee or boss, situations can change quickly. Knowing how to adapt to different situations is important to learn. Emotional intelligence helps people see how they can change their emotions or how they can read situations if and when they happen. Knowing how to handle one's emotions and make them work to one's benefit is vital to one's success.

Getting Along

There are often times that people might not get along with each other. They might struggle to work together because they do not recognize each others' feelings. Some people might be fixated on their own beliefs or values. Those who struggle to understand each other are not likely to get along. Those people will not fully recognize what is happening in each other's lives. It is through emotional intelligence that it becomes easier for a person to thrive and grow. Those who express emotional intelligence are more likely to have healthier and stronger lives where they feel more confident and compatible with others.

Emotional intelligence helps people to respect others' points of view without being judgmental and condescending. They understand that everyone has their own attitudes and that there are reasons why they feel certain ways. People who can manage their EQ well will be more likely to succeed and achieve more in life.

A Sense of Positivity

One of the greatest reasons why people are not happy is because they do not fully recognize what they are doing with their lives. They do not recognize how important it is for them to have goals and to stay confident in what they are doing.

Emotional intelligence allows a person to have a sense of perspective. Positivity particularly allows people to feel stronger about what they think and what they want to do. Part of this involves knowing one's role in work and in life. It permits an understanding of how a person has certain attitudes and what causes those attitudes and behaviors in the first place.

Chapter 4 – How Can a Person Develop EQ?

Everyone has an intriguing personality. Some people are more adventurous than others. Many people might be more excitable or interested in other people. Many might also be reserved. Personalities are different and the emotional intelligence of each person is different. An individual's personality is something that is hard-wired. One's IQ is also consistent throughout life as it focuses not so much on what one knows but how well that person can learn new things.

EQ is different. A person's emotional intelligence will vary throughout life. As the brain develops, a person will grow and develop a stronger mindset. The main reason for this is that the brain works with many parts in mind to produce a better EQ. The brain's ability to change is a key part of what makes it work.

A Basic Process

The process involved in developing a strong EQ is outlined in the following points:

1. First, the emotions are formed within the spinal cord.

The body's main senses are formed around the spinal cord as it links up to the brain. The spinal cord will feel the stresses and various other feelings that one might hold. It is through the spinal cord that the sensations in the body are felt and a person can develop the physical control one requires for living a full and productive life.

2. The sensations produced by the spinal cord will go through the limbic system.

The limbic system is a part of the brain that is near the spinal cord. This system features nerves and networks responsible for producing a person's mood. The main emotions and drives that a person holds will be triggered by the limbic system.

The emotions will entail feelings like fear, happiness, and anger. The drives focus on things that motivate a person to engage in actions. These include drives like hunger, sexual desires, and many others.

The sensations that come from one's senses will create the emotions that one feels. As the sensations are produced, the brain starts to feel a sense of comfort or discomfort depending on what one feels. The brain develops an emotional reaction before a rational action can be produced.

3. After the emotions are created, the rational brain will respond.

The brain will consider what has come about and will make a follow-up choice. The choices can be varied, but they must be planned accordingly to be easier for a person to handle and figure out.

The interesting part of the process is that so many parts of the brain are involved in producing rational thoughts. When the brain can handle all these thoughts, it becomes easier for someone to see things in a new light.

All parts of the nervous system should be strong and healthy for emotions to be formed accordingly. The goal is to allow the sensations that the brain feels to link up with each other to produce a stronger feeling that people can feel confident in without worrying about where they are going in their lives.

Plasticity Is Key

The most important part of the brain's ability to handle emotions entails its plasticity. This is a term which describes how the brain is capable of learning new skills.

The intriguing thing about the brain is that it can produce new connections in many forms. It is through the brain's ability to recognize emotions that it can handle new processes.

The connections are produced as new brain cells are formed. The brain cells must develop to produce stronger links between different parts of the brain. This includes establishing new connections that focus on managing emotions and knowing how to control them. As the brain evolves, it becomes easier for those links to be produced.

One's EQ can grow over time. Anyone who wants to improve upon one's life should see how one's EQ can move forward and become stronger over time.

The brain is an interesting organ for how well it evolves over time. If a person works hard to manage one's EQ, it becomes easy for that person to plan what can be done to change one's life and make it work.

Can One's Upbringing Make a Difference?

The theory of attachment and how people are tied to certain values or beliefs as they grow up is a very popular theory. People have discussed extensively how one's upbringing impacts how one's emotions are formed. Sometimes the emotions that people feel and their ability to identify them is a reflection of one's earliest experiences in life.

Those who are valued the most in the earliest stages of their lives are more likely to develop a strong emotional intelligence level. For instance, a child might have been taken good care of by a fine parent. A caretaker might have responded to the child's emotions during one's infancy. These include emotions relating to happiness, fear and other concerns. When a child is cared for, that child will recognize the value of emotions and how important they are to living a positive and controlled life.

Those who were led into situations where their emotions were confusing or difficult might have trained themselves to avoid emotional thoughts. A child that was not cared for might have developed worries about his or her emotions. This could have caused that child to want to separate oneself from emotions.

There is always a chance for a person to develop a better emotional attitude based on how well that person can separate themselves from their past. A person has to understand what emotional intelligence is and how one can utilize that intelligence to one's benefit.

Experience Is a Must

It takes time for a person's EQ to develop and become as strong as it can be. A person who gets into certain experiences in life will have an easier time with growing one's EQ and making it stronger. It is through consistent work and experience that a person's EQ can develop. Having an idea of what to expect from one's EQ and how to make it grow and thrive is vital to one's success in life.

It takes experience for a person to learn what one can do in life. It is through the things that a person does with one's emotional intelligence that a person can figure out what might happen in one's life. Knowing what to expect from emotional intelligence and how strong it can be will make a true difference when deciding where one will go in life.

Although the human brain ages, there is always the potential for the brain to feel restored when it learns new things and makes further connections. It might take a bit of extra time for the brain to respond, but it is a vital aspect of life that has to be used accordingly. Those who know how to grow their EQs will have a better time moving along in society and feeling stronger about what they want to get out of their lives.

No matter what someone expects from emotional intelligence, it is critical for people to see how well they can learn it. Being able to develop one's emotional intelligence is something that should work throughout one's life. Anyone who can get emotional intelligence to work as well as possible will always be in control of life without worrying about the problems that might happen.

Men vs. Women

There have been many studies over the years about how men and women are very different from one another. People talk all the time about how men act differently from women.

Conventional wisdom suggests that women develop their EQs in a way that is different from men. There are a few things of interest, but that does not mean that men and women have to use different strategies for building their EQs.

Men

Men are often better at analytical thinking. They focus on some of the more technical things in life. For instance, a man might think about what is causing a person to feel a certain way. He might look into another person's attitudes and figure out what that person is thinking based on those specific attitudes. It is through his work that he pays attention to what people are doing.

However, a man might not think too much about other people. He focuses more on himself and what he is trying to do. He looks into what he is thinking and tries to manage his life based on what he feels is right for his control in life.

Some men try to assert themselves as leaders more than women. They like to believe that their emotions are more powerful than what other men feel.

Women

A woman will do something different when she tries to help people. She will focus more on the emotional concerns that people have and express a sense of empathy toward others. It is easier for her to naturally show empathy.

A woman might also aim to be a leader, but it is not as common for women to do this. It often takes more motivation for that to happen. The female brain is more likely to become stressed, thus making it harder for a woman to decide what she wants to get out of her work and her life. Through relaxation and meditation as well as journaling, it becomes easier for the female brain to be organized and to handle the emotions and attitudes that one is experiencing.

The interesting point about what makes the male and female brains different is that it is difficult to figure out exactly why they are so different. People have chalked it up to neurotransmitter production, sexual hormones, and even how the brains of men and women are physically organized. However, they often go after the same goals of being successful and effective in the workplace.

The methods people can use for building upon their EQs are universal among men and women alike. The male and female brains are both capable of developing EQ, but it does help to look at some of the basic differences between the sexes just to see what can happen when trying to build a better mental state of mind.

Chapter 5 – The Four Core Skills

Everyone wants to do what they can to grow and thrive in their lives. They try to find ways to grow their emotional intelligence. People who know how to handle their emotions can feel positive and in control of their lives.

Emotional intelligence focuses on understanding what one can do while thinking about what others might be experiencing.

One's emotional intelligence is a combination of four vital skills that a person must have. These skills are:

1. Self-awareness

2. Self-management

These focus on the personal functions. These are based on one's self rather than the interactions with other people. A person who can handle these personal skills will be capable of managing one's behaviors.

3. Social awareness

4. Relationship management

The second two concentrate on social skills. This includes knowing how to identify what other people are feeling.

The two points of awareness concentrate on what someone sees. The two management aspects are more on what people actually do.

By increasing these four skills, a person will stay confident and positive about one's efforts when working with other people. The four should be discussed individually to get a clear idea of what to expect out of a task.

Self-Awareness

Understanding one's emotions are critical for success. The experiences one is feeling will often directly influence many things that are happening in one's life. When the right emotions are felt, it becomes easier for a person to stay active and confident in one's job and relationships with other people. Those who are not fully aware of their emotions or cannot control their emotions are not likely to succeed.

Self-awareness is a part of handling emotions. Those who have been able to attach themselves to their emotions and recognize what they are like are often capable of managing those emotions.

This goes back to the concept of attachment. When a person's emotions were respected as a child, it becomes easier for that person to value emotions and to recognize how vital they are. That person is less likely to be able to distance oneself from those emotions.

Those who are aware of their emotions will understand how the experiences and actions they have will determine the emotions they feel. People who think about their emotions and recognize how they work will feel confident and comfortable with their lives because they can see what should be done to change them.

The ways emotions can be identified include:

- Sometimes trends move along with certain emotions. One specific emotion might regularly come after another is felt.

- The physical sensations one experiences while feeling different emotions may be noticed. These include changes in body temperature, shaking feelings, and much more.

- The changes in one's facial expressions often make an impact. A person might not be fully aware of some of those expressions and how they are generated.

- Sometimes specific emotions might grab one's attention faster than others. Those emotions might overwhelm certain thoughts and make it harder for a person to take other actions.

- A person's ability to make decisions can be influenced by certain emotions. A person might recognize that it is easier to do this when specific emotions are felt. This includes changes where emotions might be too difficult to manage in some form.

A person who has self-awareness recognizes how all of these emotions will change and influence one's life.

Being Reflective

Knowing how to grow one's EQ is more than just thinking about thoughts. It is about understanding where those thoughts are coming from and why they are forming. Having a clear idea of what to do in any situation can make a difference when managed accordingly.

Those who are self-aware will be capable of reflecting upon what they are feeling. It is through reflection that it becomes easier for someone to think about certain things that are changing in one's life. Several questions can be asked when thinking about emotions:

- What emotional strengths or weaknesses does one have? Sometimes the emotions one holds are influenced by those changes.

- What does one's mood do when it comes to thoughts or actions? A person's mood might cause some changes where certain processes or actions are undertaken differently from one another.

- How are the influences on one's emotions making a difference? Every emotion has some trigger that causes that feeling to develop and persist.

A self-aware person can figure out what is causing those emotions. Knowing what comes out of those emotions is critical to understand how well certain values or behaviors might occur.

The Value of Mindfulness

One part of self-awareness that must be analyzed entails how mindfulness makes an impact. Mindfulness refers to a situation where a person can focus on emotions being felt in the present. This includes knowing how to handle those emotions right now and without judging them.

The key part of mindfulness is understanding the emotions that one feels at the moment. This includes being ready to focus on things that are happening and the positives that might come along over time.

Details on becoming mindful will be covered later in this guide. This is a process that entails meditative thought to understand what one is feeling at a given time. By making this work, it becomes easier for a person to feel comfortable with the feelings one has and it is easier to identify what is happening at any given time.

Self-Management

Self-management is knowing how to make the right decisions and choices. Those who know how to use their emotions to their advantage will be ready to make rational and sensible decisions throughout their lives.

People who can manage themselves understand what they can do when they get into tough situations. The truth is that it is impossible for people to avoid certain emotions. Those emotions can come about at any time. With self-management, it becomes easier for someone to know how to handle those emotions and to keep them from being too bothersome or hard to deal with.

When a person gets into a stressful situation, they can become overwhelmed. Take the story of Joey the retail store manager, for example. He regularly has control over his emotions and is generally self-aware of what he is feeling most of the time. He is willing to accept his emotions for what they are.

Over time, his store might become overwhelming. He might see too many things happening at a time and might lose track of the things that he needs to do to make his business active and functional. As a result, he may start to lose track of his emotions and could be at risk of making irrational decisions. He might make impulsive choices over how his store is to be run without really thinking about the potential impacts of those choices.

The reason for this is because Joey does not have the self-management skills he needs to succeed. He might know what his feelings are, but he might not be able to manage them right when they get to be too complicated or overwhelming.

Self-management is:

1. The ability to be in control of one's emotions at any time; this is more than just knowing what emotions someone has

2. The ability to adapt to any new emotions or sensations that might come about

3. Working toward achieving certain goals

4. Having a positive outlook on how well emotions and attitudes are to be managed

Knowing what one can get out of self-management is vital to success. As a person uses self-management, it becomes easier for a person to move forward and stay positive with what one wants to do in life.

People who can manage their emotions will feel confident and comfortable with their lives. They will not be at risk of choosing harmful behaviors. Self-management is about not fearing the emotions one has. It focuses on thinking clearly while managing the commitments that one has made.

The organizational efforts that come with managing one's life are vital to one's success. Knowing how to arrange one's thoughts and emotions into a series of convenient and helpful points helps anyone to go far in life and to get the most out of one's thoughts and values.

Social Awareness

While EQ concentrates on the feelings and thoughts that people have, it is also about the attitudes that other people hold. There is a need to consider what other people are thinking.

Social awareness refers to how well a person can identify the emotions of other people. This includes identifying non-verbal communication. This includes more than just how a person looks. The non-verbal cues that a person notices when engaging in social awareness could help anyone to notice what someone is doing when trying to have a better life. The nonverbal cues that people express will cause others to notice that they are happy, sad, worried, busy, or frustrated.

A person who is socially aware will express empathy. They will be comfortable with others and will understand what someone is thinking and feeling. A person is also aware of how the people in an organization are functioning. Sometimes one person's actions and feelings might indicate what everyone in a certain situation or space might be feeling.

A socially aware person will focus on the interactions that happen during a discussion. Instead of thinking about other things, the interaction taking place is the most important. They will be able to identify the experiences and feelings of another person. The movement from one feeling to another is important to explore. Those who are socially aware will communicate and empathize easily with others.

Does Social Awareness Hurt Self-Awareness?

Social awareness is not something that will cause people to lose their sense of self-awareness. If anything, a socially aware person will be more likely to be more self-aware of one's feelings. When a person pays attention to the emotions of others, it becomes easier to notice what is causing someone to feel a certain way. This, in turn, leads to a person feeling more confident in his or her own self. That person will start to recognize what causes certain feelings to happen and how behaviors can change over time. Working with a healthy sense of social awareness makes it easier for a person to be more aware of what others are doing and how their attitudes can change.

Learning from other people always helps to allow individual people to make connections. When someone's behaviors are noticed based on how they change and what someone is doing, it becomes easier for that person to be analyzed and reviewed clearly.

Relationship Management

Relationships are often difficult for people to handle. They can be complicated as people struggle to figure out what makes each other different. A relationship management plan can help people to do more with their lives and to keep from struggling to get their relationships in check.

As people understand what others are feeling, it becomes easier for their relationships to be managed appropriately. A relationship becomes stronger because everyone involved understands what is causing people to feel certain things. Those who understand the non-verbal cues that come with a relationship can succeed. They will understand what is happening in a relationship and how things can change and move forward for the better. Even more importantly, people can use their EQs to discover what they can do to make their relationships a little closer. People with enough emotional intelligence will focus on how to identify emotions and feelings that impact one's trust and positivity.

Five Vital Points

Relationship management is relevant to all people who want to produce a better working environment for all:

1. Influence

Relationship management focuses on influence. When a person knows how emotions are formed, it becomes easier to figure out what one might do. It might also be easy to see what can be done to cause a person to change certain behaviors or feelings over time. The increased influence that a person has over someone else is a part of relationship management that cannot be ignored.

2. Teamwork

People who know how their emotions are formed can work better with others. They know what to expect from others. There is also a need to keep individuals in a relationship from trying to dominate one another. Teamwork is getting people to feel better and more conducive to each other without trying to be critical or domineering toward each other.

3. Coaching

Coaching is a process where someone will educate another person in how to handle emotions and make them work in a positive way. By following a general coaching plan, it becomes easier for people to feel comfortable with one another. Coaching allows people to feel stronger and happier with what they want to do in their lives.

Coaching works best when the people who work together feel comfortable with each other. It is through coaching that people can comprehend how their lives are changing and what might happen to make things a little different and stronger.

4. Conflict management

Conflicts are difficult to handle within any relationship. Each side needs to be aware of how their emotions are changing and what can be done to keep each other in check and more likely to feel positive.

Not managing conflicts properly can become a problem. People will have to look at how they are managing their conflicts and how they are keeping them from being a threat to each other. Knowing how their emotions are developing and changing is critical to giving people an idea of how they can move forward and get their lives to become stronger and more efficient.

5. An ability to inspire

There is also a need for people to be ready to inspire one another. This includes being in touch with each other to change emotions and attitudes. Knowing what they can do will help with keeping their relationships in check. Those who can inspire another will feel stronger and more confident. They will keep their relationships moving forward while staying strong and true to themselves. The excitement that comes from being inspired and feeling confident about the self is something that cannot be easily duplicated.

All four of these parts of emotional intelligence are points that people must follow to stay positive. By using these points, it becomes easier for everyone in a situation to feel comfortable with what they want to do when changing things over time.

Chapter 6 – Common Barriers to Building Emotional Intelligence (and How to Avoid Them)

People who want to expand their emotional intelligence levels will want to do what they can to change their lives for the better and to feel more comfortable with what they want. There are often times when it might be difficult to try and expand one's EQ. Several things should be explored when figuring out what can be done to manage one's EQ while avoiding many of the barriers that can happen.

Self-Contentment

Sometimes people do not think much about how better their lives could be if they could just develop a little further. Life is a never-ending quest to figure out what one can do to become a better and stronger person. Those who work their hardest to be stronger and more thoughtful in their lives will evolve to be better people who feel comfortable with who they are and what they want to do in life.

Sometimes a person might be contented with a current situation. They might not realize that there is potential to become a better person. There is always an opportunity for someone to grow and become emotionally responsible and in control of one's life. The joys that come with being able to manage one's emotions and to read the emotions of other people are not fully appreciated until their EQ levels have increased.

To avoid the problem of self-contentment, one must think about one's emotions and to look at where they are coming from. Is there a reason why certain emotions are coming about in one's life? By looking at the attitudes one has and how certain emotions are being felt, it should become easier for a person to feel confident and capable of getting the most out of one's life.

Being Deluded

Some people constantly live in a state of delusion. A person might be deluded into thinking many things like the following:

- What things should be like

- What things might have been like in the past and what someone wishes could have happened

- Thinking that things that have happened in the past will end up guiding what comes about in the future

- Not knowing fully about what one can do to change things

- Having a desire to hear what one wants to pay attention to instead of the things that one needs to hear; this is especially in cases where a person is denying certain behaviors or actions

It is easy to become deluded by things that are happening. It is through regular exposure to certain ideas that a person might be gullible to believe in the wrong things. Sometimes a person just might think these things out of sheer convenience. A person can avoid struggling with delusions when trying to build one's EQ. These steps can be used to get rid of delusions.

1. Take a look at the source of the delusional thinking.

It might come from learning about certain things in the past or from whatever someone might be comfortable with.

Sometimes those sources are people who are trying to steer a person's life in the wrong direction. In other situations, it comes from the belief that some short-term gain is going to be good enough. A person is not thinking about the big picture or all the great things that can come about in life. The sources of the delusional thoughts often end up hurting someone and stop that person from thinking twice. In some cases, the sources are ones that do not seem realistic or rational.

2. Think about how the preconceptions are produced.

The preconceptions should be analyzed based on the types of events that might take place as a result. What might happen when one preconception is followed for too long? Sometimes a person might think that a certain event will come about over time, but in reality, it will just become difficult to make it work. When a person hears what one wants to hear, it becomes harder for that someone to have a positive mindset.

3. Look at the realism surrounding the delusional thoughts.

There might be cases where whatever it is someone is thinking is not grounded in reality. When a person is delusional, proper judgment is clouded. This includes seeing the possible outcomes of whatever is being discussed at a time.

By working with this, it becomes easier for a person to notice that some thoughts might be unrealistic. People have to understand that there is a good reason as to why something is happening.

Avoiding the Truth

Sometimes the truth can be painful and difficult to accept, but it is something that can change anyone's life. People are often worried about loss or rejection or even hearing that they need to make changes that they do not want to make.

For instance, a man who regularly smokes and has had a heart attack might be told to stop smoking. This is to keep him from potentially having another heart attack. He might not want to hear the truth. He might like smoking and he is not willing to pay attention to all the lectures about a heart attack. Therefore, he will just keep on smoking while tuning out people telling him not to do it.

The man in the example does not have the emotional intelligence needed to accept what is happening in his life. He feels that he is just fine and that he isn't the one that needs to change. There is a good reason why he is not hearing the truth. The man is not paying attention to the truth because he is distorting what he is hearing. He might be jumping to conclusions. He might hear someone saying "You aren't doing right for yourself," but he could interpret that as "You are a terrible person." That man might try to keep the status quo and avoid the people who are trying to help him because he thinks that those people are doing more to hurt him.

This problem can be avoided by working with a plan to talk about what is being said. A person could ask for clarification about the truth and what that person is saying.

For the smoker in this story, he could talk with the people who are telling him that he is not doing well for himself. He could ask for confirmation and clarification over what is happening with his life. This could result in him discovering that he can get rid of the smoking habit by following some simple instructions for better living.

Being able to accept the truth is important for one's emotional intelligence. It keeps that person from trying to deny things that are truthful. It is through the truth that a person will have a better and more productive life.

Being Upset

One of the strongest feelings is becoming upset over whatever is going on in one's life. The troubles that a person might have can be great. Anyone could get upset over various things. A person has to watch for what can happen after being upset. Whether it is unhappiness about an event not going some way or from something not being as useful, it is vital to observe what could happen at a given moment.

1. Remove yourself from the situation.

Part of building one's EQ is being removed from whatever is causing certain behaviors or feelings. The situation must be analyzed from a distance. This includes looking at why an event is happening the way it is.

2. Find out what is causing something to happen.

A person needs to look at why something is happening and what is making it happen. A good way to find out what is happening is identifying the problems.

3. Be willing to accept things that have happened.

The most important thing to do when overcoming being upset is to accept what has come about. A person should be willing to acknowledge that something is changing because of certain things that have happened.

Trying to Feel Perfect

Many people who want to resist changes in their lives might do so because they think they are perfect as they are. They feel that their lives have moved forward for the best and that they are confident with what they are doing. They do not see much need to change or to do things differently. When a person feels perfect, their judgment starts to become clouded. They feel that nothing wrong is going to happen and that everything will be smooth sailing from here on out.

What that means is that a person is not going to think about what can be done to make good changes. It is impossible to feel perfect all the time. There will always be a chance that a person will have certain thoughts or values that might clash with what one might normally think. Those thoughts might cloud one's judgment and make it harder for that person to notice that there are many things that can be done to change one's life and to try and feel stronger.

Perfection is not something that happens easily. It takes effort and works for a person to have a stronger and more productive life and to feel better about the things they are trying to do. One can never be perfect when trying to build one's EQ. It is through trying to get closer to perfection that the art of growing EQ is all about. Although that perfection is not possible, having a better EQ at least gives that person the feeling that something positive is happening in life.

The Act of Self-Sabotage

Conventional wisdom suggests that a person will stay positive and try to find ways to change one's life for the better. There are also times when a person might be afraid of what will happen in life. Although a person might be happy with what they are doing, there are times when a person might want to continue with what is happening even when it is not going as well as planned. It is a frustrating aspect of life.

Self-sabotage is a process where a person keeps him or herself from accomplishing more and to be more productive. There is a reason why people with low EQ levels engage in self-sabotage. A person might not be emotionally prepared to handle some of the changes that can come in one's life. This could come from some worries that a person has about what can be done.

Here's a story about Jennifer, a woman who has been working at a retail job for nearly twenty years. She has been making a great deal of money and has great job stability and benefits, but there are many other job opportunities that she could consider. These include jobs that use the skills she has developed in her retail job. These job positions might be new environments and duties, but there is a greater potential for added pay and even more benefits than what she is getting right now.

So, why would she self-sabotage herself and not look for one of those jobs even if they are better? She might be afraid of what will happen when she leaves her current position.

Jennifer might think that when she gets into a new position, she will not know what she can do there. She might not be able to handle the success. Maybe she is worried that she will fail in that new job.

The best thing she can do to resolve this block is to look at her feelings. She needs to look at how realistic her beliefs are or where her emotions are coming from.

By developing the emotional intelligence needed to succeed, it becomes easier for a person to move forward and stay strong. Having the emotional intelligence one requires makes it so any thoughts or fears can be analyzed a little further, thus helping to find what is right versus what is false. A person with a high EQ will avoid self-sabotage by thinking about the real benefits that come with certain actions and not about the outlandish worries that have no substance.

Blaming Other People

A related part of self-sabotage is not only keeping the self down but also be blaming others. When things do not go one's way, that person might try to pass the blame to someone else.

Blaming others is an act of self-sabotage in that a person will try to hold others accountable for one's own failings. For instance, a man might be upset that he did not get a job that he wanted. He might blame various factors for why he did not succeed. He might think that other people were better or even that there are laws that he perceives to be working against him.

However, a high EQ person would avoid blaming those others. They would realize that although there are many problems and issues, it is the self that is responsible for an issue above all else.

The man in this example would have to look into himself to see what has happened in his life. He would have to review how he presents himself and what he was doing to get that job. A closer look at his efforts might reveal a few flaws that he had or some mistakes that he committed. At this point, he will stop blaming other people and start blaming himself.

He will stop self-sabotaging by looking into why he is doing something. He will start thinking more about what he can do to fix the problems that he has.

Emotionally intelligent people know that there is always something about themselves that cause them to fall apart and fail. They know that blaming other people is not only immature but also unrealistic. Trying to find reasons to blame others for their failures or for preventing them from getting where they want to be is only hurtful to the person doing the blaming.

Feeling Harsh Emotions

Some of the more difficult emotions that people have could be dangerous and risky. These include problematic emotions like fear and anger. Such harsh emotions are tough to live with because they make a person intense and difficult to get along with. Even more importantly, those emotions might be based on irrational thoughts and hostility toward other people.

These emotions can be controlled by looking at what causes them to develop. Sometimes a person might need to rest for a bit and think about whatever is happening. Understanding the issues one is encountering can help figure out what problems one has.

The most important reason for getting beyond these harsh emotions is because it is easy for the brain to become preoccupied. The problems that occur when some of these emotions are felt can be dramatic. When a person feels something intense, the brain starts to lose focus. Everything one is thinking about will be centralized around the harsh emotions that one has developed. The anger caused by an event often makes life a challenge. These are problems that must be addressed to keep people in control of their lives.

Fears of Uncertainty

People are more content when they know what to expect. They appreciate it when things are going along smoothly. It is easy for people to be scared of what might happen in the future. They can become so frightened about the future that they are prevented from moving forward and being effective in whatever they want to do.

This is related to self-sabotage, but in this case, a person is not actively trying to hurt oneself out of fear. Rather, they are just trying to actively avoid anything that might entail change. Knowing what to watch for when it comes to the future and how it might change is something that must be explored in all its detail.

For instance, a person might want to travel to certain places, but that person stays with the same routines. A person who wants to travel to Washington DC might be interested in going to the same spots and doing the same things every time. That person is not interested in going to any of the unique sites that the city has to offer because they do not feel comfortable with anything new or different. Maybe that person does not feel confident about their ability to take in new experiences. Of course, there is also the general sense of comfort that comes with enjoying certainty.

People should face what they are afraid of. A person with a strong EQ will know how to talk with someone who is afraid of things that may come about in the future. Knowing how to reach a person who is worried about what might come along in life is always helpful.

A person who builds upon one's EQ will start to realize what is causing feelings of fear. Those worries could be unrealistic and harmful to one's life. Knowing how to manage one's EQ and to get beyond some of those thoughts and fears is vital to one's general success.

Living a life filled with fear is never a good thing. It is through a person's fears that it often becomes a challenge for a person to live. Those who are afraid of things in their lives will not be positive about what they want to do or how they are going to emotionally and mentally evolve. A person needs to recognize what can be done to create positive and meaningful changes in life without struggling to perform or move ahead in that life.

All of these points in this chapter are issues that can keep people from building their emotional intelligence. Those who know what they can do to avoid these blocks and to build upon their emotions in a positive manner will succeed and go far in life. Having a plan for building EQ is critical to stay strong and productive with whatever they want to do.

Chapter 7 – Identifying Impacts on Emotions

People choose to complete various tasks and manage their emotions in numerous ways throughout the day. Those who have a high level of emotional intelligence are more likely to know how to keep their emotions in check.

There are many points in life that will directly influence the emotions that someone has. Knowing how to identify these points is essential to building one's emotional intelligence as these aspects relate to how emotions are produced and how far they can go in one's life. Working with assistance to keep such emotions in check and safe can make a true difference if managed right.

A Degree of Separation

The first point that will influence one's emotions is how well a person is able to separate oneself from other people. People with high emotional intelligence levels will see themselves as being separate from others in an environment. They understand that their experiences are different from what others have had.

The fact is that there are many people in an environment does not mean that every person is going to have the same attitudes or beliefs. Sometimes the attitudes or hopes that a person conveys will be different from what another person might be saying or feeling at a time. The struggles and issues that come along with what someone might be thinking can be different from what someone might have been considering.

For instance, there might be multiple people in a doctor's waiting room. Janet is experienced in going to the doctor and knows that there is nothing for her to be afraid of. She is aware that it is through the doctor's services that she will feel better and healthier. More importantly, she knows that doctors are always there to help her and give her the best advice possible.

Meanwhile, David might be worried while waiting for the doctor. He is uncertain about what will happen as he has not been to the doctor very often. He feels that the doctor might tell him bad news or might do something painful. He isn't aware of how a doctor wants to help him and that anything that might be harmful is done for his greater good; this includes taking a blood sample.

Janet has a strong level of emotional intelligence and is not going to let David's fear impact her. She knows that her experience is separate from what David has. David could develop his emotional intelligence when he sees that a doctor's visit is not as painful or difficult to bear with as he might think it is.

What if Janet didn't have the emotional intelligence that she currently has? In this case, Janet would become worried and fearful of what is going to happen. She might be worried because of the fear that David presents. His attitudes might cause her to start fearing what will happen in the doctor's office. It is through Janet's emotional intelligence that she is able to avoid this problem.

This is a point about emotions that shows that it only takes a few moments for people to respond to certain situations and to become worried about what can happen in their lives. The Betari Box chapter later in this guide offers more details on how emotions might spread from one person to another in any environment.

Perceived Threat

Emotions are often influenced by the threat that someone might experience. In the doctor example, Janet has positive feelings because she does not see a threat in a doctor's visit. She only sees great things coming out of it.

David is on the opposite end. He feels that the threat that comes with a visit is high because there might be a situation where someone might give him the bad news about his health.

Janet is stronger on the EQ front because she knows that the threat involved with the doctor's visit is not all that great. She feels that her emotions will be kept under control and easy to manage.

The perceived thought that comes in a situation may be based on experience or on what someone hears from other people. The truth is that there is no way one experience is going to repeat itself several times over. Knowing what can happen in life and how to make it all work accordingly is critical to avoiding perceived threats in any situation.

Anxiety

Anxiety is another concern that directly impacts one's feelings. A person with a strong level of emotional intelligence will not likely be influenced by feelings of anxiety. A mind free of anxiety is capable of figuring out rational thoughts while coming up with smart ideas and useful beliefs. Those who are anxious might be at risk of harm.

Janet is not anxious in this situation, but David certainly is. Janet is not worried about what will happen because she has an idea of what to expect in a certain situation. David's fears are greater and he is not comfortable with what could happen.

It is only natural for people to feel anxiety at some points in their lives. Many people recognize that their emotions can be intense. Sometimes those people are feeling unhappy or upset with their lives. In other cases, it is about wishing that they were in a more familiar setting. Anxiety can be controlled in some manner. A high EQ person will recognize the anxiety that is happening and find a way to eliminate it from one's mind. This includes knowing what can be done to keep that anxiety from being a dramatic threat that does more to bother the mind and keep it from working as well as it should.

Feelings of Trust

Trust is vital for emotional intelligence as those who trust others will not begin to feel irrational or have illogical thoughts. It is through a sense of trust that someone might feel comfortable and start to make certain decisions.

The trust that is produced in this situation can work in two forms. First, the trust may start with one's ability to feel confident in one's own competence. This includes an ability to handle certain tasks and to make a good impression on other people. Second, trust entails working with other people. Part of this involves hearing what other people have to say and what makes their values or ideas worthwhile. It is through the trust that is produced by people can think more about what is happening in their lives and what they can expect.

People with a high emotional intelligence are willing to find people that they can trust. They will notice when someone is ready to do things the right way or if someone is honest. There might also be times when a person is willing to trust one's own feelings. People with a high emotional intelligence are ready to trust what they are doing and are not afraid of what might occur in their lives. The positivity that comes through certain actions and ideas can make a bigger difference than what one might expect.

In addition, there might be times when a person leads someone down the wrong path. The trust produced might be dangerous and harmful. A person might convince other people that he or she is worth trusting, but in the end, that person will not do anything for others. This is an unethical point about emotional intelligence that must be explored, although there will be a discussion on ethics and EQ later in this guide.

The most important part of trust is that it is what guides people to make decisions that they are comfortable with. It is also about how people will side with others in certain situations. Take a look at a couple that might have been married for a long time. What has caused that couple to remain together for forty, fifty, or maybe even sixty years? That couple will have stayed together because they trust one another. Trust is more important to them than money or health. It is about knowing that they are going to be with each other through the good times and bad in life. They will feel better knowing that each is not going to be judgmental or hard on the other.

Having a broad sense of control over one's life is vital for success. It is through this control that a person will understand what can be done to get ahead in life and to stay active and functional. It is only through that control that a person can become successful and likely to thrive and get somewhere in life. Knowing what to do with control is a point that all people must be ready to work with if they are to succeed and do more in their lives.

Feelings of Attachment

Everyone can become attached to certain things in their lives. For instance, Bob might feel attached to an old car that he has. Bob might have had the same car for twenty years and really loves it. He knows that it needs an extensive amount of repair and that it constantly struggles to run, but he feels too attached to that vehicle. He does not want to part with it even though it is clearly the thing he needs to do.

Bob does not have much emotional intelligence at this point because he feels that he cannot just get rid of that car even if doing is the right thing for him to do. He knows that he needs to get rid of that car and get a new one that will not break down all the time. But he is attached to the old vehicle and he cannot just get rid of it. He wants to keep that vehicle working for as long as possible.

If Bob had a better level of emotional intelligence, he would notice that he does not have to keep that car forever. He could get rid of that old car and find a new one that has more features and will run better. Bob might even notice that it will cost less for him to get a new car and keep it working normally than it would for him to keep trying to get that old car repaired.

When Bob's EQ improves, he starts to remove those feelings of attachment that he has toward certain things. He starts to notice that there is a logical reason why he needs to get away from things that could be troubling or problematic for him.

Feelings of attachment are not always produced based on trust. While trust entails people feeling confident in one another and emotionally positive, the attachment is about trying to stay with something regardless of whether it is the rational thing to do. In other words, trust is about respect while attachment is about self-involvement.

A high EQ person will understand that attachment is not always the right thing to enter into. There will come a time when someone has to get away from something that a person is addicted to and wants to keep on working with. A low EQ person will not fully understand what is going on in one's life and will try to find ways to avoid situations where that person will have to let go of something that they are attached to and feels they are incapable of living without.

A Sense of Commitment

Everyone is committed to the tasks that they complete in many ways. Some people might be bent on completing tasks in a specific way. They might not want to veer off course when trying to get their work completed. Others might be willing to remove themselves from commitment. They could be ready to take on new challenges and try things a little differently from what they are normally used to doing.

Let's go back to Bob, for instance. His goal might be to have a car that can run for 200,000 miles before it has to be scrapped. He might be so adamant about that goal that he is willing to keep the old car that is twenty years old and has 160,000 miles on it. He might try to keep that car running to reach that goal and is willing to get to that 200,000-mile mark no matter what happens.

Bob would have a poor EQ at this point because he is too fixated on one thing. He does not recognize that there are

71

other things that he can do. Better yet, he does not notice that he could still get to that milestone if he bought a used car recently that has thousands of miles on it but is newer and better built. Such a car would be more likely to reach that special milestone even though it would take a while.

Things would be different if Bob had a better EQ. He would be flexible enough to know that there are many ways for him to get to that milestone. One of the solutions is to buy a used car that would be easier to maintain and is built to last longer. He might notice through reason that newer vehicles are easier to care for and built with better materials that aren't likely to break down. He might go from a 20-year-old vehicle with 160,000 miles to a four-year-old vehicle with just 50,000 miles. He also knows that the vehicle can last for a while and that he can enjoy his vehicle without struggling with extreme expenses for trying to get that old vehicle running.

This example relates to commitment - sometimes a person might be too fixated on a single goal that they not aware of the more reasonable and sensible alternatives. Changing one's attitudes or efforts for reaching a goal is best for keeping one's life in check and easier to do.

This does not mean that commitment is a bad thing. There are many logical activities that a person can be committed to. A person may be committed to having a good job or being in a strong marriage. A high EQ person will look at the commitments they have and decide if they are worthwhile or if there are problems with them that should be addressed. There is a need to look at those commitments and see if they are meaningful enough to continue to move forward and be viable points for one's life.

Knowing all of the things that can impact one's emotions is vital to figuring out what someone might be doing with living. Those who have a better EQ will not be likely to have these blocks get in the way. Anyone who wants to have a better life needs to know what to expect from these problems and how they can be resolved before they get worse.

Chapter 8 – Reading Body Language by Emotion

Everyone takes various physical positions throughout the day. Most of these are ones that people are not fully aware of. They are many natural responses to situations. These positions make up a person's body language.

The body language that a person expresses should be the most important thing for people to notice when trying to see how their emotions are working. This part of emotional intelligence focuses on recognizing what is causing a person to feel a certain way. By reviewing a person's body language, it becomes easier for that person to be supported and assisted in some fashion.

A person with a high EQ will recognize the body language of another person easily. This includes knowing what a person is thinking without having to hear a single word. If anything, body language reveals more about a person's emotions than anything. A person could say anything that might contradict one's real feelings. It is through the physical body language that a person's true motives or feelings will come into play.

Each emotion that one has can be identified by several physical points. Anyone looking to build upon their emotional intelligence will have an easier time with doing so by looking at some of these physical considerations.

How Are These Motions Produced? (And What Do They Mean)

It is important to know that body language operates as an extension of the things that people say, what they think, or the actions they do. A person with a high EQ will recognize that many forms of body language will cause people to act in ways.

The intriguing part of the motions produced is that people often are not aware of how they are changing their body positions. They simply respond to things based on what they see and how they feel. Sometimes it is easy for a person to get into one of these positions. This makes it all the more essential for a person to look into how these motions come about and what might cause a person to act in specific ways based on what they want to exhibit or express.

Body language is often triggered by mental impulses. Sometimes these come about as a person is trying to hide one's actual feelings.

Body language can be studied through a practice known as kinesics. It is a study of how body movements and shifts in one's physical stature might influence what a person would say or do at any time.

There are a few points about body language that can be seen through kinesics:

1. Many body movements are signals of something a person wants to say. Although they are often silent, they can be translated into certain ideas. A person who shakes one's fist might be showing a sign of anger, although that might be joking when the voice or context that the shaking takes place is considered.

2. Other movements reinforce the things a person says. When someone says "on one hand," that person puts his or her hands in one direction. After saying "on the other hand," the hand go in the opposite direction.

3. Body language dictates how far removed a person might be from a concept or if that someone is linked to. For instance, the speed of one's movements might reflect the rhythm of what is being discussed. That speed is also a sign of how removed a person is from something provided that the person is not that excited or intrigued about something.

4. Emotions might be noticed based on how the body is curved or how fast it is moving.

5. Physical tensions may be released through one's body language. It is through this that a person can safely express true feelings without getting verbally upset.

The main point about the emotions one has is that they can be very intense or even muted at times. It is through one's body language that it can be easy for a person to grow and evolve as a person. Body language must be explored based on how well things might change in one's life and what struggles a person might enter into based on what is happening.

Let's take a look at individual emotions. The next section is all about how emotions might develop and what causes them to become significant.

Looking at Emotions

The emotions that a person has throughout the day can be varied. A person will go from being happy to sad to joyful to upset in just a single day. It is often difficult for people to figure out what they can do in their lives because they are going through so many emotions each day.

People who want to look into what others are thinking should take a look at the emotions that are being produced.

A high EQ person will observe certain emotions based on nonverbal communication as a means of developing empathy with someone and to tailor one's conversation. By noticing these emotions, a high EQ person will become easier to trust.

A high EQ person will recognize that there are reasons why people are speaking in certain ways or why they might be difficult to work with at times. When a person is emotionally intelligent, they can use another person's body language to their advantage.

Anger

Anger is a feeling that can be easy to notice based on the aggravated sensations that one has throughout their body. Sometimes a person might be talking normally, but in other cases, the anger might be hidden. Anger can be quickly noticed by how agitated or frustrated someone appears to be:

- An angry person might look worn out or tired. This could be due to a higher heart rate.

- A person's posture might appear tight - hands on the hips in or the arms folded. At this point, the person is trying to keep looking stern.

- Sweating is a telltale sign of someone being angry. This is often a byproduct of a higher heart rate.

- Clenched fists show a person trying to keep one's anger hidden.

- The eyes might be fixed on one particular item. It could be what someone has said or just some object that someone is frustrated about.

The best way to look at these points is to see what is causing a person to feel frustrated. The nonverbal movements relating to one's anger should be compared with what is causing those movements to develop. Knowing what is causing certain actions to develop makes a difference when seeing how a person's life is changing and what attitudes are being shown.

Happiness

Happiness is always something that shows that a person is comfortable and confident. Not all people who are happy will have smiles on their faces or a skip in one's step. There are several nonverbal aspects of happiness:

- The body might feel relaxed. A person is not feeling tight or rigid in some way.

- The arms and legs appear to be open and relaxed. That person is not trying to keep one's distance at this juncture. Rather, that person is showing that he or she is confident around other people.

- The eye contact might be a little more prolonged or consistent. At this point, a person is willing to show one's interest in a subject or concept.

When someone notices that a person is happy, it is only second nature to try and figure out what is causing that person to be happy in the first place. Knowing what is causing this happiness and finding a way to make it last is an important point for anyone to explore. In some cases, a person might use the findings that come out of an investigation and find a way to become happy oneself.

Interest

Sometimes a person might be a whole lot more interested in something than what he or she suggests. This could be due to the language that one is using. Someone could act more inquisitive or curious about what is happening. In most cases, interest might be some non-verbal cues. A person with a strong EQ will notice some of these non-verbal triggers:

- Someone might move a little closer toward something. This could include not only walking toward an item but also leaning forward in one's seat.

- Wide eyes are a good sign that someone is really paying attention.

- A fixed glance also suggests that a person is really interested in something and wants to see what makes it special.

The interest that a person has could be about anything. The best thing to do is to look at what someone is more interested in based on how excited one's body language might seem. Certain triggers or concepts will cause a person to become more excited at certain times than at other times.

Anxiety

Feelings of anxiety can be a real problem for people to handle. Anxiety often shows that a person is worried and fearful over things that might come along and change. Some people do well to hide their anxiety by simply accepting the things they enter into, but there are people who might be nervous and fearful over what might happen.

A person who is anxious might show many physical changes:

- A person will be restless. They might move around and pace or try to think of other things. Those efforts might be unsuccessful due to the ongoing worries someone has over trying to do things the right way.

- Rapid breathing shows how a person is fearful or nervous.

- Sweating might be easier to spot here than it is when someone is angry. An angry person is just frustrated; anxiety just makes it harder for a person to want to go forward.

The important point about anxiety is that it is not always something that people will notice right away. Looking at the smallest physical cues helps to understand what is going on in one's life.

<u>Sadness (and How a Person Hides It)</u>

Anyone who feels sad will not be motivated to do much. That person might be afraid of what could happen.

Sadness can be a sign of many things. It might be a sign of when a person is unhappy with things not going the way one wants them to be. In some of the more significant cases, sadness comes from a person feeling stressed or even depressed with many things in life. The worries that can develop can be dramatic and could be a real threat that keeps a person from being productive or able to make friends.

Several things can be noticed in a person who is sad. These are some of the more commonplace signs, but the things that a person feels will vary by each situation:

- The eyes appear to be downcast and fixated on the ground. It is as though someone is upset and preoccupied with something problematic.

- The mouth does not appear to be moving upward.

- The body looks sluggish and worn out. A person could start drooping downward.

- Even the speed at which one does something should be reviewed. A person might be rather slow or sluggish.

The second part of sadness is how a person might try to hide their sadness. People are often worried about exposing their sadness and will then do what they can to keep their feelings of sorrow from being noticed.

Many people who are sad will do what they can to keep themselves from feeling that way. The nonverbal communication is commonplace among those who are depressed and struggle with many issues in their lives. In particular, many people will hide their depressed feelings out of fear that they will be judged. They are not actively trying to get the help that they need. In fact, they might not even know that they need help.

Part of building one's EQ should be looking at what people can do when they try to hide their true feelings. This includes knowing what people might do as they aim to keep themselves from having their feelings or thoughts exposed.

There are many nonverbal communications that suggest someone is hiding feelings of sadness:

- Any attempts to express happiness through non-verbal communication might not seem genuine. A person could try to move one's body too fast or engage in quick motions to show one's energy.

- The physical actions a person expressed when someone leaves or something stops quickly changes. This could be a feeling of abandonment.

- A person might be trying too hard to express feelings of love for someone. This is a sign that a person really wants to talk to someone and doesn't want to be left alone.

- A person might try to get physically close out of fear that someone will leave.

It is critical to observe these actions in a person who is sad. They may be signs that there is something emotionally wrong with a person and that they need help.

Surprise

Sometimes a person might become surprised with certain things that are happening. A feeling of surprise suggests that something is happening that is very different from what a person might have expected to find. A feeling of surprise will have many physical cues:

- The eyes appear to be wide open. The person is curious as to why something is so different from what was expected. The eyebrows might also appear to move upward.

- A person might feel as though everything one had known has changed in some way. This creates a sudden feeling where someone might start to question other things that came about.

- A person's mouth might be open or at least relaxed. This is another sign of someone not knowing what to think about what is happening.

It only takes a few moments for feelings of surprise to kick in within one's mind. Knowing when these feelings occur can help anyone to see what is causing someone to feel surprised. Making connections between certain events and those feelings helps build one's EQ by recognizing what is triggering those feelings.

Another point to discover is what is causing that surprise. Observing the body language that develops after someone is surprised is vital to see how a person might feel. An individual might be relieved from a surprise or might become worried.

Embarrassment

Everyone likes to prove that they are right or are smarter than others in a room. What happens when a person is not right? What if that person is proven to be completely wrong about something that was promoted or discussed?

Embarrassment is not a feeling that people want to have, but it is something that might come about in any situation. There are many non-verbal cues of embarrassment that anyone with a high EQ can notice:

- A red face is a sign of someone realizing that he or she is incorrect.

- A person might try to look away from others. This is due to that person knowing that he or she was wrong.

- A person will try to avoid direct eye contact out of a fear of judgment.

- Someone might try to smile, but that smile might be forced.

It is through the non-verbal cues that feelings can be identified. Knowing how certain emotions are coming about through body language can be one of the most essential parts of emotional intelligence that anyone could ever use.

Chapter 9 – Body Language According to Personal Distance

There is another part of body language that is vital for EQ development that all people should review. This refers to proxemics, a concept where a person's physical or personal distance from others might say more about their feelings.

Anthropologist Edward T. Hall reviewed proxemics as a concept about how people might stay close to one another or become removed based on what they are feeling or thinking. A person who is physically closer to someone might have certain values.

This point is vital for emotional intelligence in that a person needs to look into how far away a person is when communicating to understand what that someone is doing. More importantly, a person can use proxemics to figure out how close he or she should be to someone else.

For instance, Billy might know when it is fine for him to get a little closer to someone. He might have a high EQ and would understand that he should not be within a few feet of another person unless it is with romance in mind.

What if Billy had a low EQ? He might get too close to people when talking to them, thus making himself look intimidating to others. This action would be done without him having any romantic intentions.

This is symbolic of what it might take for a person to have a healthier and stronger life. When a person has a high EQ, that someone will know when to keep space from others. This includes knowing that there is a time to be near someone and a time to step away and not crowd a space.

Understanding Proxemics

Proxemics was developed by Edward T. Hall as a measurement of how people divide themselves from others. It is about understanding how each person has their own personal space that needs to be recognized. The concept suggests that when a person is physically closer to someone, the relationship between the two is stronger.

Take the example of Paul and Nick. The two of them play on a baseball team. Paul and Nick might enjoy each other's presence. Paul might sit next to Nick while on the bench. They might fist bump, chest bump or give each other a pat on the back when they do things well. They are physically close because they know they are competing with the same goal to win. The two of them are great friends and teammates and therefore will stick together from a physical standpoint. They feed off of each other rather well.

Now, let's say that they weren't feeling close to each other. Paul might resent that Nick is getting more playing time on the field. Maybe Nick feels that Paul is a stronger contender who is going to steal the spotlight away from him. The two might not be as close to each other at this point. They might sit far from each other while on the bench. Maybe they will not acknowledge each other's accomplishments even when they win games.

A high EQ person will notice in this situation that the two players are not getting along with one another. A coach who is emotionally intelligent will notice that the increased distance between the two is a sign that they are not compatible, thus leading to a desire to figure out what is causing those two people to act in the way that they do.

The Four Main Zones

Edward T. Hall stated in his research on proxemics that there are four distance zones that may be explored among people. The four zones are divided based on how far they might be from one another. The four zones are:

1. Public Distance Zone – At least 12 feet

The first zone is the public distance zone, a zone that entails a person speaking to someone from at least 12 feet away. A public distance zone is for people who are talking to large groups. In this case, all the people in that group are treated as a singular individual entity. This is a point that is commonplace among people who regularly engage in public speaking.

Many people are comfortable with public distance zones. They might feel that they can talk with others en masse and not worry about their individual emotions. All those people are one collective entity.

Let's go back to the baseball team of Paul and Nick. The manager might use a public distance zone to talk to all the people on the team. The zone is used to let everyone know that certain commands or requests are being given to everyone.

The public distance zone works particularly well for romantic purposes. It is fine for someone to look at a person of interest without going too far. Sometimes the target might be flattered about being noticed. When that person gets a little closer, the target might become uncomfortable with the situation and fearful of what is happening.

It is perfectly fine for a person looking to build one's emotional intelligence to start out with a public distance zone when talking or interacting with people. The key is for someone to move into a relationship gradually. Knowing one's space between others is critical for starting a good relationship while eventually moving closer to something positive.

2. Social Distance Zone – 5 to 12 feet

The social distance zone moves in a little closer and is for people who want to engage in a conversation but are not fully aware of one another or what each other has to bring to the table.

For the baseball team, people on that team who are not familiar with each other might use social distance zones. They might address themselves from this far at the start because they want to introduce themselves but are not fully comfortable with those people just yet.

The social distance zone allows people to be comfortable with each other while they get to know one another. It is a non-intimidating approach to communication that works well for people who are going to be together in a space for a certain period.

An even better way to describe the social distance zone is to think about everyday actions. For instance, Paul might go to a grocery store to pick up some things for his team. He might stop at a bank and ask a clerk to withdraw money from his account. After that, he will be talking to a cashier who will help ring up the purchases he just made.

The social distance zones that Paul enters into are established as he will be with those cashiers and tellers for a brief bit of time but will still need to conduct business. The social distance zone is ideal as Paul is working with those people but is not going to be too familiar with them.

When building one's EQ, it is important to be gradual when entering the social distance zone. It is fine to do this in many cases where one-on-one interactions are needed. However, this works best when one is doing this with someone who that person is going to interact with regularly for a longer period of time.

3. Personal Distance Zone – Around 2 to 5 feet

There are often times when people might get a little closer to one another. The personal distance zone is where someone is about two to five feet away from a person. When people are within personal distance zones, they are showing that they trust each other and recognize the needs they have.

The personal distance zone is where a person is willing to talk to someone about anything. It is here where people might feel confident and comfortable with each other. While in a personal distance zone, people will do things like shake hands, talk with each other, and make more intense gestures.

Paul might establish a personal distance zone between many people on his baseball team. He will have that zone with Nick, the manager, and anyone else who he feels close to. Paul knows that he can talk with his teammates, coaches, and others on the team about what is happening with that club and how they are competing. More importantly, Paul is showing that he is comfortable around all those people.

The personal distance zone is the space where people will show like each other. Paul might not have liked Nick much when they first started playing together, but that can be chalked up to how the two were not familiar with each other. After being on the same team for a while and getting to know each other's strengths and weaknesses, the two would eventually get into the personal distance zone because they feel comfortable around one another.

4. Intimate Distance Zone – Less than 2 feet

The intimate distance zone is the closest zone. This is a situation where people will get directly in touch with each other could physically touch one another.

While Paul and Nick might be close while on the baseball team, they are not going to get into the intimate distance zone. It is fine for them to give one another a pat on the back, a high five, or another physical sign of approval when they do things well on the field. But the intimate distance zone is very different from that.

The intimate distance zone is about being people direct and personal with each other. It is often reserved for family members and for romantic partners. An interaction in this zone might entail an intense hug or a hold onto one another. Of course, sexual actions would qualify as being in the intimate distance zone.

This is a vital part of keeping one's distance in that those who can manage their distance from others in a healthy way will have more control over their lives. The biggest problem people often have with the intimate distance zone is that they can abuse it to intimidate people. When a person gets into this zone without knowing much about the person whose zone is being infringed upon, the target will feel intimidated.

For instance, a police officer might interrogate a suspect. The officer will get physically close to the suspect during the investigation. The officer will do this to lower a person's defenses thanks to the added pressure that the suspect will be subjected to. By producing this intense attitude and pressure, it becomes easier for a person to feel a need to respond to a threat.

People who are very close to others are often doing more than just being intimate and friendly to one another. They may have other motives.

How Proxemics Relate to EQ

The proxemics in a relationship is vital for emotional intelligence as it shows how well people recognize each other. When a person is physically close to someone, that person knows the target and is willing to be intimate with that individual. This could come from sharing secrets, expressing emotions directly or even engaging in sexual activities.

The distance between people can also be a sign of intimidation. Those who do not know each other well will feel fearful and concerned about any interactions that take place here. It is through the interactions involved that people might feel comfortable or confident in what each wants to do.

A person should do more than just notice how far apart or close individuals are. That person must also watch one's own distance. A high EQ person will know that when meeting someone for the first time, it helps to add a bit of distance.

Proxemics is vital for people to review when emotional intelligence is considered. There is a need for people to look at how well they are interacting with each other and how well they can talk with other. Knowing how to work with proxemics can make a difference when finding solutions for managing one's life the right way.

Chapter 10 – Reading Body Language

There are many instances in life where one's body language might be a challenge. These include cases where a person is overly defensive or otherwise not willing to pay attention.

A person with a strong EQ will know how to identify these points and how they might work. Not only that, a high EQ person will understand that certain physical positions mean specific things, thus allowing that person to be more mindful and to avoid getting into certain problems regarding how various positions are made.

People who want to build upon their EQ should see how body language works in these situations. By knowing how to identify a person's emotions, it becomes easier for someone to get in touch with that person and to respond correctly. More importantly, it establishes a sense of empathy where the defensive person will discover that there is someone out there who cares about the needs that person holds.

The identified emotions in a case will help a person to notice what is happening in a situation. This includes working to understand some of the problems that a person has. At this point, a plan may be devised to figure out how to reach people or how to resolve the problems that someone might encounter.

Defensiveness

People are often willing to defend themselves in any way they see fit. Sometimes a person might be so adamant about something that he or she does not want to be proven wrong. That person might insist that he or she is right and will not budge from that opinion.

This part of managing emotions does more to hurt the mind. It closes off one's emotions and ability to recognize what others are doing.

The appearance of defensiveness also expresses the following:

- A person might feel nervous and frustrated over something.

- That someone might be stressed and does not know what to do to resolve a certain problem or situation.

- A person could also be angry. This might come from things not going in the way one might have wished they could.

There are several things to notice when finding someone who appears to be defensive and not ready to make any real changes to one's life:

1. A person's arms are folded.

2. Any facial expressions produced are either halted or slight or are otherwise muted.

3. A person could be turning their body away from other people. This is a sign that someone really does not want to talk to other people or be near them.

4. The eyes are cast downward. A person could have a downcast attitude that is keeping that someone from feeling confident.

It might be difficult to reach a person because they have some beliefs that are very hard to shake or might otherwise clash with what is being introduced. Knowing how to reach a person at this point and to have a better sense of communication is a necessity for getting a relationship to move along.

A Lack of Engagement

A business meeting can be valuable, but there are often times when someone might not be paying a lot of attention. This could include one person who is really not into what is being said. That person might start to look disoriented or not amused by something.

The best managers are high EQ people who know when certain people in the workplace are not paying attention or are not interested. Those managers will know that they need to talk with other people in the workplace and see what it is that they want.

Meanwhile, high EQ employees will know that to show a sense of interest in a meeting, they have to avoid signs of disengagement. They know that to show that they are valuable workers, they have to express clear signs of interest in anything that is happening at a given time. Knowing how to express such feelings and attitudes is vital for going far and doing more in the workplace.

The signs of a lack of engagement include the following:

- The person is not sitting upright in one's chair.

- The head appears downcast. Although this could be a sign of being tired, it is more than often a sign of someone just waiting for an event to be over.

- That person is also gazing at something else in the room.

- Physical stimuli include fussing with something or toying with a pen or other item. That person is trying to keep him or herself busy while waiting for the meeting to be over.

- Something could be done to try and occupy the time. This includes doodling or drawing on a notepad. Perhaps a person is writing something, but it might not actually be noted from the meeting but rather just random stuff one would write down for the fun of it.

In most cases, the lack of engagement is a result of a person not having much interest in a speech. It is up to the speaker to figure out why this person is not interested so that they can get in touch with the person and try to find a way to get that person to pay attention and appreciate whatever is being said.

How Does Someone Engage That Person?

The person who is not interested in something should be consulted after noticing that the person is not engaged. When expressing one's emotional intelligence, it is important to not be judgmental. Rather, the need is to ask someone why he or she is not paying attention nor has no real interest in whatever is being said at the time.

Several things can be done to engage in a person and to see if that someone is ready to communicate:

1. Ask a question of that person. Ask if that someone is interested in something. If that person isn't intrigued, see about creating a link between something that person likes and whatever the topic at hand might be.

2. Gauge a person's interest by asking about what that someone wants to get out of a task. Talk about something like what might make a project or event interesting to someone.

3. Ask a person to contribute one's own ideas. Allowing that person to add some value or thought to the process can make a discussion more interesting to everyone involved.

The general goal is for everyone in a situation to feel comfortable and confident with what is happening. The most important thing is that this part of EQ entails more than just showing a sense of empathy. This also includes allowing a person to feel more confident and to be a little more open to ideas.

Frustration

There are times when a person is frustrated or worried about things that are happening in one's life. The frustration can be a challenge, but it is important to notice what might be happening to one's body. The physical signs of frustration include the following:

- A person is sweating or feeling hot. This could happen because they have too many things on their mind.

- Someone might be quiet or reserved. This is a sign that a person is worried about things and is too busy being fixated on them.

- A person would also look downward while pacing or standing still. The person is trying to come up with a mental strategy for resolving the issues they have.

Frustration is a concern that is not always going to have people being physically active or agitated. It often involves how a person is worried about life and would rather be somewhere else trying to resolve the situation.

No one should be worried about cases where people might engage in certain physical actions. Each action is natural and will come about at random. When working with particular physical stimuli, it will be critical for people to understand how their attitudes are changing and what is causing them to think in certain ways.

Copying Body Language

A unique phenomenon people often come across in conversations involves cases where people are copying one another's body language. For instance, a man might uncross his arms during a conversation. The other person listening to him will do the same shortly after.

When a second person copies a first person's body language, it is a sign that the two people are on the same page with one another. They are starting to develop a bond with each other. The second person might notice that the first is no longer being defensive as the arms are no longer crossed. Therefore, the second will do the same thing and stop being defensive. The two people are now in a situation where they can trust each other and pay attention to what one another has to say.

As two people copy each other's body language, they show that they have a mutual sense of admiration and respect for one another. They are not going to be defensive with each other.

Copying body language works well in business discussions. When two people are doing the same thing, they are showing that they can negotiate with each other and come up with good ideas and compromises.

There is also a dark side to this part of body language. Although copying body language is a sign of comfort and positivity in a situation, it is also could be a sign of a person mocking the other. For instance, one person who is frustrated or upset might copy certain movements in a fast or halted stance. This could be to mock or insult the other person.

The key is to look at how natural the changes in body language happen. When the changes move smoothly and naturally, the people in the conversation will notice that there is nothing to be worried or concerned about. The people on all sides of the situation will feel relaxed about the conversation in question.

The most important point is that the copying should be done unconsciously. In most cases, the changes in one's body language in response to others comes not out of purpose but rather because of the unconscious brain having some changes in its attitude.

Those who copy other peoples' body language while doing so in a peaceful and natural manner are ones that will be easy to work with.

Chapter 11 – Reading Body Language by Haptics

The ways a person's face and other physical features move and change are important to understanding when developing one's emotional intelligence. It is also vital for a person to analyze the body language by looking at the gestures someone might be making. Those gestures can range from simple hand movements to more intense movements.

One particular form of body language that deserves to be analyzed entails haptics. This is a practice that involves how people communicate with each other by touch. A person with a high EQ will understand what people are feeling based on the physical contact they make. This could be anything from a pat on the back in the workplace to random acts of intimacy in the bedroom.

People often associate haptics with sexual actions or anything related to romance. This is understandable because people are closer to one another if they are in a strong relationship with each other. It is important to understand why people engage in haptics. High EQ people recognize the meanings of certain touches. People should be aware of what they are doing when using certain motions to interact with people in ways that are appropriate for the situation.

Social Touching

Social touching is a basic form of touching that happens between people every day. Some of the more common forms of social touching include the following:

- Patting someone on the back

- Shaking hands

- Giving someone a high five

- Brushing off someone's clothing when that person sees something on it

These forms of social touching are people interacting with each other gently. It is through social touching that people show that they care while also expressing the feelings they have without accosting each other.

It is fascinating to see what makes social touching work. The key point for managing social touching is to only do it when needed. A high EQ person will recognize that touching works best when trying to offer a compliment or a sense of gratitude or care for a person. When the touching is done for other intentions, it produces a lack of trust and a fear of what might happen.

Intimate Touching

Some haptics are intimate touching and relates to how close people are to one another.

The haptics that a person has, in this case, can include:

- Hugging and kissing

- Touching personal parts of the body

- Sexual intensity

- Touching a person's body for longer than just a few seconds

Some of these intimate touchings can be in public like a simple hug that takes a second or two. Other actions like a long open-mouth kiss or anything that might be sexual should be done in a private setting. When high EQ persons are intimate, they are showing that they are close to each other and that they want to be together.

Even more importantly, people might think about the deep feelings that others have. A high EQ situation would involve looking into how intense the intimate touching is. If the touching is very strong and takes more than a moment, it suggests that a person has a stronger emotional or sensual relationship to a person and wants to hold onto that link for as long as possible.

Haptics is in play when a person notices certain motions and physical interactions. The touching that goes on during a communication between people should be explored and studied based on how well people interact with each other and what they can expect out of a situation.

Chapter 12 – Surface Message vs. Deeper Message

There are many ways for people to identify messages. It only takes a few moments for people to look at the messages they come across to see if they are worthwhile or if there are certain concerns that have to be considered.

An emotionally intelligent person will know what is happening with people when asking them questions. The questions being posed in a discussion can be complicated. The best way to look at these points when developing one's EQ is to look at surface messages and deeper messages. A surface message is like the part of an iceberg that is above the water. It is a small surface, but it does show something valuable. A deeper message is like the bottom part of the iceberg that is under the water. The deeper message will be a reason for why the surface message was introduced.

Surface Messages

A person will have to look at the surface message. An emotionally intelligent person will start noticing that there is something being said. This could include one of many things:

- A person might express an opinion. It could be being happy, afraid, or worried.

- A statement of interest may be communicated.

- Some surface messages focus on things that people see. They might observe something and tell people to look at whatever they are interested in.

The surface message is a vague statement. A high EQ person will notice this and will then want to probe deeper. For example, a person might say "I am very happy right now." The high EQ individual would respond by saying, "What are you happy about?"

It is here that the high EQ person wants to get an answer to something. That person will want to discover why someone is happy but will be doing so in a peaceful manner. The person who made the first statement is opening themselves to further questioning. However, the questioning should not be too intense or complicated. The discussion should instead be simple and calm.

Deeper Messages

Although a surface message says quite a bit about what someone is thinking, that message is not as important as the deeper message. An emotionally intelligent person will do what it takes to discover the deeper message. There is always going to be a reason why a person feels a certain way.

Here's an example of how a deeper message might work:

- When a person says, "I am worried," the deeper message is what that person is worried about. The specifics about one's fear will be discussed at this juncture.

- When a person expresses something interesting, a deeper message will involve why that person has an interest. Someone would say "I really like this art painting" and would also have a deeper message that states why that person feels the way they do.

- A goal could be established to discover what will be done to get there. When someone says "I want to win the game," the deeper meaning would be "Here's what I am going to do to win."

A high EQ person will have to look at the deeper message by asking politely about the things in the message. The meaning could be anything relating to how much effort someone is putting into a task or how happy someone might be about one's line of work. Whatever the case may be, effort must be put into finding the deeper meaning. The high EQ person should not pressure the other person into revealing one's reasons for doing something. That high EQ figure has to be friendly and cautious while respecting one's personal space. The questioning should be done so that a simple straightforward answer can be given at the target's comfort. When a person says, "I'm feeling great today," it is fine to respond by saying "Why are you feeling so great?" By doing so, a friendly sense of conversation will start up. The people being talked to in this case will feel comfortable knowing that the high EQ individual wants to get an answer without being too demanding.

Although the surface message is helpful, it is the deeper message that is more important. Easing a person from the surface message into the deeper one is very important.

What's more important about this is that it shows a person is not willing to assume things. A low EQ person will just assume that a person is feeling in some way but not explore why. A high EQ person will know that there is always a good reason why a person feels in a certain way.

Chapter 13 – Managing Self-Awareness

It is time here to look at how self-awareness works and what makes it a dynamic part of emotional intelligence. By using self-awareness, it becomes easier for people to stay with plans for handling their lives and knowing what their goals are.

Emotionally aware people are more likely to succeed. Self-awareness is critical to understand what one can do in life. It is through self-awareness that a person is able to figure out what one's emotions are all about.

Self-awareness is knowing what to get out of one's work. This includes understanding not only emotions but also what causes them to develop.

The concept was introduced in 1972 by Duval and Wicklund in their book "A Theory of Objective Self-Awareness". The authors of the book state that self-awareness is comparing one's current behavior with other points. It is the need to review one's behaviors is to see how well certain standards and values in life can be organized. When people are self-aware of what they are doing, they will know more about what might be of value to them.

It is through being self-aware that people know what they can do to produce the best habits so they can handle throughout their lives. People who are self-aware know all about where their emotions are going and what they will get out of their lives. People can also take control of the things that they want to go forward with.

Self-Awareness

When people hear the term "self-awareness," they immediately associate it with being familiar with what is happening in one's life. Part of this includes knowing the things someone is doing at a time and the efforts that person is putting into one's life. While these points are all vital aspects of self-awareness, this is an aspect of life that entails much more:

1. One's personality is easier to review.

An individual personality can be complicated. Every personality has its own traits and trigger points that cause someone to act in a certain fashion. It is through these personality points that a person is able to grow and thrive and become a functional and effective human being.

2. The strengths and weaknesses that one has.

Everyone has individual strengths and weaknesses. A person might do well with getting people to feel happy but might not know what to do when someone is dealing with emotional trauma or other significant problems.

A self-aware person understands how one's emotions are formed and what that person works best with. This can include a person figuring out what to do in the future when trying to change one's emotions and actions or to see what should be done to make positive and worthwhile changes that can last. Anything someone can do for success is critical to understand.

3. It involves looking at the thoughts and beliefs that one has.

Every person has a series of thoughts or values that can make a real difference in one's life. It is through those values that a person can make the right choices in life. The things that someone might consider or look into can make a vital difference to anything one wants to do in life. Every thought process can vary based on many factors. Some people might think about things based on historical events or experiences they had in their lives. Others focus more on what might happen.

4. Motivations are critical to self-awareness.

Every behavior and emotion is triggered by some motivation. A person who is sad might feel a need for sadness because of how difficult their life has become or that it is difficult to go somewhere and do more. Others are motivated to be happy because they know that positive things are on the horizon. Maybe these great things might be a pay raise at work or the satisfaction that comes with a job well done.

The motivations that someone has will directly influence how well that person can move forward. It is through motivation that a person will feel encouraged and ready to do whatever it takes to move forward and be happy.

This part of EQ should involve each of these aspects to help someone recognize everything that goes into one's emotions and how they are formed.

A person who is self-aware will understand other people and know what one can do in life to be around others and to stay positive or in control of one's life. By working with plans to be self-aware, it becomes easier for someone to succeed.

Benefits of Self-Awareness

Self-awareness is vital for being comfortable and confident with what one wants to do in life. Having an idea of the emotions being felt is needed to allow plans to be made for the future and how well the mind and body can be controlled.

Self-awareness lets people explore more about their lives and what they want to achieve. It is through this that people will understand what they can do to benefit their lives.

The benefits that come with self-awareness are:

1. Being self-aware allows a person to see things in the present.

There are always reasons for why certain things are happening. Those who are self-aware know that there are many reasons why things happen and they know how to take advantage of what occurs.

People who are not aware of their emotions will act irrationally and ask themselves later why they were doing certain things. More importantly, not being aware of emotions clouds a person's judgment and makes it harder for that person to use their intelligence.

2. People are aware of any influences or biases that they might have.

A person needs to find ways to correct the biases they have. There are always influences in life. Knowing about the things that impact one's life can be critical to see what should be done to have a stronger and more productive life. These influences can come in many forms. Sometimes they are prior experiences in one's life or what prejudices one has. It is important to understand these problems and views one has and to then review how they might be clouding one's judgment or ability to make decisions.

    3. How emotions are produced need to be understood.

Knowing what causes emotions to occur is vital for building emotional intelligence. Those who know their emotions will see what is happening in their lives and what they are doing. Knowing what makes emotions start could be an influential point to be analyzed.

    4. People who are self-aware will find corrective solutions for managing their emotions.

Self-awareness is recognizing situations that cause certain emotions and knowing how to control those emotions. This is high EQ thinking.

Create an Objective

The first thing for a person to look at is one's objectives in life. People who know how to manage their lives and put in the right efforts will succeed in life.

Being objective is looking at the facts. This includes seeing what is going on right now and how those things are changing one's life. There are many things that can be done to produce objectivity.

    1. Look at the perceptions of an event.

A person might perceive that someone is good or bad because of a certain activity or that there is something outside an area that is changing things.

2. Review the past.

Everyone has things in their lives that stand out to them in some fashion. Many people are confident about themselves thanks to certain jobs they completed in the past or how they had strong relationships. It is vital to look at the past to get an idea of what is causing certain emotions to occur. Sometimes emotions might develop because of positive or negative events that took place in one's life. These emotions can be troubling at times, but they have to be analyzed. It is through a full review that a person can develop a clearer understanding of what one is doing in life and why.

3. Look at the changes that have happened.

Everyone's life changes in some fashion. There are things in one's childhood that might cause a person to act in certain ways. That person might have grown up and started having interests in certain things. There might be a few things of interest that a person continues to enjoy and appreciate today.

An emotionally intelligent person will look back at how one's emotions have changed and how trigger points for those feelings have evolved. A full analysis is needed for understanding what someone is doing and why.

4. Honesty is the best policy when taking an objective look.

Being objective is being honest. Those who are honest will be more likely to know what they are doing with their lives and where they are going. It is through honesty that a person will be positive and happy with what one wants in life.

Slow Down

People these days are living their lives at a breakneck speed. They want to do things quickly and without problems. That speed makes it harder for people to live their lives. They make mistakes and errors in judgment. They don't know what they are thinking in many cases. They are often going to rush through what they do.

It does not take much time for people to lose control of their emotions or thoughts. Those who are not careful with what they are thinking or feeling might become angry or hostile. This only hurts relationships with other people. As a person struggles with those negative emotions, the overall situation can become worse and harder to manage.

A vital part of self-awareness to follow is to slow things down for a moment. There is always some reason as to why something is happening and it is the emotions one has that will dictate what happens in a situation.

Slowing down allows a person to become more aware of their emotions. As the brain becomes relaxed, it is easier for the person to feel in control. Anyone who knows what is happening will be able to handle the situation.

A few steps can be used when trying to slow down:

1. Be aware of a negative emotion occurs.

Such feelings include the emotions of distrust, anger, annoyance, or disappointment.

2. Isolate that emotion and figure out what it is attached to.

The emotion might be linked to a single person or a certain event. Be specific when looking at the event in question.

3. Identify why that emotion came about. See if there is some back-story associated with the emotion and what is causing a change.

Sometimes the emotion one feels is unrealistic and unnecessary. That feeling might be hard for someone to manage and take charge of.

In many cases, the emotion might come about due to a negative memory. This memory might trigger feelings that are not comfortable.

4. Figure out if something else can be done.

The root cause of the feeling should be explored. This includes taking a closer look at why a feeling has come about. Knowing what is causing that feeling to occur is a necessity for keeping one's mind under control.

Being ready to slow down when a negative emotion happens is critical for keeping one's life under control. It is through this that a person becomes aware of certain emotions while figuring out what can be done to keep those issues from being worse than they might already be.

Daily Self-Reflection

A long day at work or school can be a real burden especially when they are in situations that they are not always excited about or willing to do.

Self-reflection is a practice where a person looks back at the things that have happened in a day. It is through this that someone can determine why certain emotions were felt or why specific actions took place throughout the day. When someone reflects on one's life, it becomes easier to understand what might be coming along in the future.

Self-reflection only takes a few minutes in a day. To do this, a person can relax at the end of the day and think about the things that occurred.

Journaling can work at this point. Just sitting with one's thoughts can be worthwhile too. Whatever the case, a person can spend about fifteen minutes at the end of each day to figure out what they have thought about and what activities they did.

Write Down Goals and Plans

Everyone has their own goals and plans for their lives. Self-aware people understand that their goals and plans often determine the emotions that they feel.

The goals someone has can be planned by working with a few steps:

1. A series of larger goals can be produced at the start.

2. These goals may be broken down into smaller goals to be achieved sooner. These smaller goals may contribute to the larger ones.

3. A timeframe for those goals can be decided, but that is optional.

4. The goals one has can then be compared with the emotions that one feels based on those goals.

Connections between certain objectives and feelings can be established at this point.

Knowing how to get more out of these connections can make a world of difference if managed well. The best part of this exercise is that a person can get one's priorities in order. Knowing how to manage these priorities is vital for figuring out how life is to move forward and what should be done to keep it going well and in check.

Work With a Journal

Journaling is a perfect exercise for building self-awareness. The practice is writing down things that one did in the day and what someone might want to do in the future. Journaling allows a person to express their raw emotions. Such emotions can be a challenge to live with, but they must be explored.

Anyone who writes in a journal can do so with uncensored and unfiltered thoughts. These include feelings that are causing someone to act in specific ways. Keeping the journal open and direct is critical to helping people see what they can do when getting their lives to move forward and feel a little stronger and more comfortable in any fashion.

Meditating

Meditation has long been utilized as an activity for a person can get in touch with their personal thoughts and values. Meditation involves being in a quiet place and thinking about the day. This is a mental form of journaling. Meditation provides a person with the opportunity to look back at one's day and see where someone might be going with life.

Talk With Others

Having an outside opinion is always a good idea. Although a person's own self-awareness might help, it is even more important for a person to find out what others think. This includes working with people who are co-workers or supporters. People who talk with others about who they are what they are doing with their lives can make real changes in their lives. They need to know from others about what is happening and what they are doing to make themselves appealing to others. Having a plan for managing one's life is vital for success and for moving ahead with one's life.

This works best when the people who are being contacted are those whom a person can trust and appreciate. The best people in this situation should be good friends who are honest and willing to be direct. These include people who appreciate someone but aren't going to try and influence. The key is to find an honest opinion so it becomes easier to make changes to one's behavior.

It is up to a person to get outside opinions from others to become more aware of what they are like. Just going by one's own opinions or values is not good enough as it could be easy for someone to skew one's opinions about views about what that they are doing.

On the Job

A related strategy to use for self-awareness is to ask for feedback while on the job. Getting feedback helps people to realize what they can do better. Many businesses perform special tests on their employees to see what their attitudes are and how they can complete tasks on the job. This includes looking into how they are emotionally structured.

Feedback may be provided to employees by their managers or other people who conduct the tests. The feedback provides information on how well people can manage their emotions. The details provided can make a real difference when figuring out what can be done to grow as an individual.

The feedback given by an employer can be useful provided that the manager in question is fair and honest. A person has to offer enough feedback that is simple and useful.

Organize Values by Importance

Everyone has their own values or desires in their lives. Some people want to have strong jobs while others want to enter into the best romantic relationships possible. Emotionally intelligent people know that the things they appreciate the most have certain values attached to them. They understand that there is a sense of importance that can be attached to everything in their lives.

Life values are used by high EQ people to decide how they should prioritize to guide the behaviors and choices that one makes.

For instance, a person might feel that one's health is very important. That person will then do what they can to improve their health and keep it in check. This includes finding ways to get more exercise or to eat more healthily.

Those who can arrange their values and keep them in check will see that there is nothing for them to really fear in their lives. They will know what they want to get out of the work that they put in and that they can keep it moving forward as well as possible.

The number of values that a person can have is endless. Each of those values should be sorted based on what might be more important to someone and how those concepts are to be introduced accordingly.

Review Goals

Every person has goals that need to be met in life. The goals that people might hold when moving forward in their lives can be varied. Some people might have multiple goals. They want to go to many places and want to get the most out of whatever they want to do. It is through the goals that people hold that they explore what they are doing and how far they can go ahead and get the most out of their lives.

A self-aware person will review their goals and how they are prioritized. This includes a careful look at how goals being set in life are organized and what a person can do to reach them in a smart and efficient manner. By looking at one's goals and seeing how well they are laid out, it becomes easier for a person to be successful and have a good life.

The goals should be organized based on how important they are. Sometimes one goal might be more important than another. Maybe a person's immediate health is critical in that they need to lose weight now before finding a new job. When a person manages their health, they can then move on to finding a better job that might offer more pay and benefits.

A long-term plan for goals can be utilized as well. This includes looking into how much time it would take for those goals to be realized.

A person has to avoid multi-tasking. Although multi-tasking could help people to do things quickly, it might cause others to lose track of their goals and to eventually fail to complete their tasks as well as they could because they are trying to do too many things at once.

Tests for Reviewing Self-Awareness

There are some tests that people can use and are not intended to be all-knowing or definite. They are made to give people ideas of what to expect out of their lives and what they wish to do. A test should help with understanding what someone can do with life and how well it can be managed based on what can be done to be more self-aware.

An interesting part of tests for self-awareness is that many businesses or organizations will devise their own tests. They create these to make it easier for them to review what their employees or other people around them are like. There are a few professional tests that might work even better. Such tests are designed to be easy to follow and will consider many points relating to one's self-aware attitudes. Knowing how these tests are run and what to get out of their results is a necessity for seeing what might come along when trying to move forward with a better and more productive life.

The Myers-Briggs Test

The Myers-Briggs Test is the best test to consider when looking into self-awareness. Although there are countless tests for people to use, this is the most prominent one that people can follow. The test focuses on what people can do when managing their attitudes and feelings.

This is a test that focuses on identifying a person's personality. The Myers-Briggs Test is based on a test that was produced by Carl Jung and Isabel Myers-Briggs. The focus of the test concentrates on things such as:

- Extraversion or introversion. A person might focus on outside things or on internal struggles.

- Sensing or intuition. People often focus more on things based on what they see. Others aim to interpret. They do this to figure out what things might happen.

- Thinking or feeling. Many people focus on logic and thought when making decisions. Other might look at the people involved and might consider some of the special circumstances surrounding certain events that are taking place.

- Judging or perceiving. People often think about the structures that they see in the outside world. People often think about what others are doing, but some might judge others. Many people might look for meaning behind situations.

These four points are combined according to the Myers-Briggs Test. The questions in the test include many that focus on the attitudes that a person might have. Some of the questions involved are:

- Are you late for your appointments?

- Do you enjoy fast-paced activities?

- How involved are you in the tasks you participate in?

- How easy is it for you to get excited?

- Do you focus on reason or feelings when making choices?

- How well do you plan your actions? Do you think about them ahead of time or are you trying to change things on the fly?

- How do you complete your tasks? Do you do things quickly or do you take your time with them?

- What do you feel like after you talk to people? Are you relaxed or comfortable when talking to them?

- Are you a social person or do you prefer to do things on your own?

The questions in the test are important for people to review. The test can be taken online, but there are also some online service providers that produce professionally organized tests that might be more accurate. Sometimes the tests involved might include fifty or more questions.

These questions are designed to help people analyze what their personalities are like. This helps with self-awareness in that a person's emotional intelligence will grow as more is known about the type of personality they have.

iNLP Test

The Institute for Neuro-Linguistic Programming has developed a test that focuses on understanding how self-aware a person is. The test is issued through the iNLP website and is provided to professional organizations looking to gauge the people who are in the workplace about how they are living their lives.

Ten categories are used in the iNLP test. A person is given five options on each of these categories to give a full description of what one is like. These ten categories are as follows:

1. How people hear and see things

2. The general worldview that someone has

3. Positive and negative beliefs about the self

4. Life values

5. Cases where values one holds clash and compete with each other

6. Anything that triggers stressful feelings or worries

7. Cases where one's parents or guardians are influencing one's actions; this is for adults as sometimes a person's parents might still dictate one's thoughts

8. Limits one has; these include both literal limits and anything someone perceives to exist

9. Cases where self-sabotage has taken place

10. What to expect out of the future

By answering the questions, a person will reveal what they are thinking and why that person is living life in a certain way. It helps to understand how aware that person is about one's life. The test is designed to help people understand the points that might evolve in one's life and how it can move forward.

A Vital Note

As useful as these tests can be, it is critical to avoid making too many generalizations. Although a test provides a good idea of how self-aware someone is, no test should ever be used as the answer to what a person is like. Rather, a test result should be a good review that is understandable.

Self-awareness is a part of life that no one should ever ignore. It is through self-awareness that a person will become capable of identifying what they want to do in life. Being aware of one's feelings and what is causing those feelings is a point about emotional intelligence that makes a difference.

Chapter 14 – The Value of Self-Regulation

The emotions that people feel throughout the day are often challenging. A typical person will run through a gamut of emotions relating to many issues and challenges that can come along. These emotions can be everything from happiness to sorrow. It is through emotional intelligence that a person is able to grow the ability to regulate those emotions. Self-regulation is a concept that focuses on what people can do to grow and handle their emotions.

A person who can control their emotions will understand what it takes to keep certain emotions from persisting or lasting too long. Part of this involves finding ways to resolve troubling emotions and to prevent them from being more difficult than necessary

Three Key Attributes of People Who Can Regulate Themselves

It is through self-regulation that people will understand what they can do to change their lives for the better. There are three specific attributes that people hold when they understand what they can do to regulate their attitudes and emotions.

1. People have the will to reflect on what they are doing.

When a person reflects upon life, they start noticing why certain behaviors or attitudes are produced. These emotions and feelings might be stronger when one's EQ is very high.

The thoughtfulness that comes upon reflection allows a person to be at peace. The person will accept that things are happening in a certain way. After that, some effort may be necessary to change one's emotions and attitudes.

2. A person is willing to accept the uncertainty of the situation.

There are many ways a person might be willing to accept that things are not always going to work the way they want. A person who doesn't understand self-regulation will not be ready to accept some of the problems that can come along in life or that there are unexpected things that can happen.

Self-regulation is being able to adapt to whatever changes might occur. This includes knowing that whatever might occur in a situation, there is always going to be something worth noticing.

3. Self-regulating people have a sense of integrity in their lives.

It takes an effort to say no. People often say yes to everything in their lives because they don't want to let people down. Some might do so because they are afraid of what will happen if they say no. A self-regulating person will hold the integrity that one needs to refuse things if it is not to their benefit. Integrity involves being honest and ready to stick to the principles one holds. These include moral beliefs that one has. It is about helping others, but it is also about helping them while working with the abilities one has.

For instance, a person with a strong EQ will realize that there is nothing wrong with saying no if they are being asked if he or she can come into the workplace on one's day off. A person who is very busy with other tasks in life might feel pressured. That extra work might hurt their ability to complete certain tasks in the workplace.

With a strong EQ, that person will know that they are not going to get into trouble by saying no. That person understands that other people are not going to be upset over some of the things that they are denied. Someone with a high EQ will realize what can be done to keep their life in check without being problematic. It is through one's EQ that is becoming easier for someone to make the right decisions and changes in one's life.

Why Is Self-Regulation so Important?

Self-regulation is critical to one's life for many reasons:

1. Self-regulation allows a person to become reasonable.

Knowing what will happen in life versus what probably will not occur is vital to one's success in life. When emotions become easy to regulate thanks to a high EQ, a person will know that there are many realistic considerations to consider. When a person is reasonable, they will make rational and smart decisions. They will not fall into difficult traps where it becomes easy to make the worst possible decisions. More importantly, the reasonable attitude that one has will be fair and sensible.

2. Self-regulation allows people to be a little more competitive in the things they do.

Competition makes it difficult for people to try to keep going in today's society. It is through competition that people are able to make decisions and keep their lives intact. Self-regulation helps people to become more competitive.

A person who can regulate one's emotions will know what to expect from most situations in an environment. Part of this includes being ready to change certain actions or values based on what might be happening in a certain situation.

3. Impulses will be easier for a person to resist.

Impulses are often difficult for people to control. They can cause a person to want to do things without thinking. A person might act quickly based on the first things that pop into one's mind regardless of whether or not those things in question are sensible or worthwhile.

When a person has a sense of self-regulation, it becomes easier to be focused on a task at hand. There is less risk of a person to be sidetracked.

More importantly, a person will keep one's emotions in check so it becomes harder for them to fall prey to some impulse. Most of these impulses are produced by rash decisions or actions. Getting into these sudden actions can be a real burden due to a person not knowing how to manage one's thoughts. Those who can regulate their emotions will go further and have more help to keep their minds in check.

Self-regulation is a specific part of emotional intelligence that no one should take for granted. Being capable of managing emotions and keeping them from being difficult to control is vital to have a better and more effective life.

Chapter 15 – Being Reflective

A high EQ person will be reflective of what is happening in one's life and how a person might be acting in some way. It is critical for someone to be reflective and ready to acknowledge what is happening with one's life in general. It is through reflections that it becomes easier for people to know what they can do and how they are going to go about with their lives.

Naturally, people might assume that being reflective involves looking back at one's life. Reflectiveness is often associated with getting older and looking at what someone has done and how a life has been lived. Being reflective also involves looking at oneself in the present.

Five Critical Goals

There are many things that can be done to help a person go further and to keep certain attitudes and issues under control.

1. Be ready to look at the good and bad things about the self.

High EQ people recognize that they are far from perfect. If anything, there is no such thing as a truly perfect person. Everyone has their faults and flaws that need to be considered. Sometimes these problems come about because people are not willing to think about the bad stuff in their lives.

Part of being reflective involves knowing that one is not perfect and that it is impossible to truly be perfect. Knowing how to look at these problems and manage them right is vital to one's success in life.

2. Be aware of the reasons why someone is trying to appear perfect.

The most common reason why people often try to make themselves look perfect is that they are afraid of being exposed as jokes to others. They might feel shame over how difficult it is for them to show their true selves. Sometimes people refuse to accept their problems and will not reflect on who they are out of fear. They might think that if they are perfect people will admire them.

A high EQ person will understand that many of the reasons people try to appear perfect are that they have high expectations. Some people feel that when they are not perfect that they might be shunned or criticized. But those who are willing to accept that they are not perfect will not deal with lots of stress or pressure in their lives because they know that they can keep themselves in control without problems.

3. Look at what emotions are felt as a result of trying to be perfect.

Some people might feel stressed or fatigued from all the things they try to do. They might become worried because they know it is hard for them to make positive changes in their lives or to make their lives move forward as well as they might hope.

Many emotions might come about during the quest to change one's life. For instance, a person might feel pained or frustrated with some of the things that one wants to do with life just to be perfect. Maybe a person might be scared of what will happen if they are not perfect.

Are those emotions realistic or rational? It is key to see what is causing these emotions to develop and if they are rational or if they should be resolved or corrected by changing one's attitudes or values. Knowing how to change can make a real difference when managed right.

4. Be ready to ask about why these feelings are developing.

There are often things that could have happened in one's past that are causing someone to feel a certain way about the things. These points might cause a person to feel scared or frustrated in some fashion. It is understandable as to why people might feel certain ways, but it is even more critical to see where these feelings are coming from. Are these feelings occurring because of past events in one's life? Maybe they are from someone being scared of something that is changing in life.

5. Be ready to stop denying the truth and to start accepting reality.

Emotional intelligence is about understanding that there are always going to be things in one's life that cannot be changed. These include things relating to the attitudes one holds and how they are addressed. People who do not accept the truth are often likely to fall apart and not know much about what they can do to help themselves.

High EQ people are not afraid of the present and of realities. They know that there are many things in their lives that have gotten them to where they are today. They will look at these points and see how they are influencing their lives with an emphasis on understanding what can be done to change one's life for the better.

It is through one's reality that life can move forward. Trying to come up with some fictional reality that is more positive than what is really happening is something a low EQ person would do. The fiction will only mask what is really happening. Having control over one's life and what is being done to make it run in some fashion is vital for moving forward and getting something to work in one's routines and attitudes.

Being reflective is a necessity for life. It is critical for anyone who wants to go do more with life to be reflective and capable of understanding what one can do to have a stronger and more controlled life.

Chapter 16 – How to Become Mindful

It is easy for some emotions to be overwhelming, but those who are mindful will be more likely to stay confident and positive with one's life. It becomes easier for anyone to manage emotions when one is mindful and aware of what is happening in one's life. When a person is mindful, it is second nature to recognize the emotions one is feeling.

Mindfulness is critical to emotional intelligence because those who are mindful will be capable of staying productive. A mindful person understands that certain emotions are being felt and that they should simply be recognized for what they are. That person will be more likely to feel positive and will not feel as much stress.

It is through mindfulness that a person can develop emotional intelligence by knowing what makes life worthwhile. Knowing what is great in life and how emotions are formed is vital to getting the most out of life.

Mindfulness has its roots in Buddhism, but it is a value that can be utilized by anyone regardless of one's upbringing.

The Main Goal

The general goal of being mindful is to accept emotions and experiences as they happen. This includes accepting emotions that are painful. A person will have to not avoid or ignore certain emotions as they are formed.

Mindfulness works well for emotional intelligence as it concentrates on gaining perspective toward the emotions that one feels. A person will recognize that emotions are being formed with certain reasons or intentions. That person will not be likely to feel a lack of confidence because they will recognize what is going on in life and how it is changing.

The most important thing is that the thoughts will become more rational. Because a person is willing to accept certain thoughts, it becomes harder for those thoughts to be irrational and difficult to manage. The risk of self-defeating thoughts will become minimal.

Other Benefits

There are four other great benefits of mindfulness that are relevant to the quest for a greater emotional intelligence:

1. A person will become more satisfied with life by being mindful.

Even the most negative and difficult emotions will be rewarding when someone is mindful. By accepting emotions, it becomes easier to recognize all the good things that come out in life. When a person is standing in a flower garden, that person will stop feeling stressed and start to feel at ease. They will recognize that there are many beautiful things in the world worth stopping to look at. By having less stress, it becomes easier for a person to organize one's life and to have an idea of what one wants out of it. This, in turn, causes that person to feel satisfied and confident with whatever one wants to gain out of life.

2. With mindfulness, a person will become more in the moment.

Being in the moment is critical to living well. When a person is aware of what is happening at a given moment, it becomes easier for that person to stay focused on certain tasks or to recognize rational things that can be done at any time.

People who live in the moment will be less focused on stressful things. They will not be overly concerned or worried about their self-esteem or whether they are being portrayed in a positive light. Those who are less stressed will also develop better relationships with others.

When something is happening in real time, it becomes harder for a person to be fixed on upsetting things that could happen in life. When a person thinks about the things that could happen in a situation, it becomes harder for that person to make smart choices. By thinking about the negative outcomes that might occur in an event, it becomes easy for someone to be obsessed with things that might change. It is harder for a person to know what to do in a situation. In the worst cases, the situation gets worse because that person will end up making some questionable decisions based on what could happen and not what is happening in the present.

Sometimes those negative thoughts will come from not only what might happen but also what has happened in the past. A person might worry about a decision because of some negative thing that took place in the past. When a negative thought permeates one's mind, it becomes harder to make good decisions.

3. A person's physical health may improve.

Those who are not mindful will not likely stay healthy. When a person thinks about current emotions, it is easier for the body to feel relaxed. The risk of ongoing stress from thinking about too many negative things can be a problem. When a person is fearful and uncertain about one's emotions, it becomes easier for physical issues to occur. These include such problems as:

- Increased stress

- High blood pressure

- Frequent pains

- General feelings of restlessness; this includes an inability to sleep properly

- Some gastrointestinal discomfort

- Added risk of heart disease

By being negative, the mind focuses on too many things that might be difficult to live with. Even worse, a person might forget about one's body and try to take care of the little things in life. This results in a person becoming unhealthy and unable to handle one's body and mind well. All that preoccupation will do more to hurt the body than anything else.

When one is mindful, the fears and worries of what has happened or what could happen will be kept in check. This, in turn, reduces the ongoing worries that someone might have.

4. A person's mental health will also improve by being mindful.

Mindfulness helps relax the brain and keep a person from feeling stressed or frustrated. By concentrating on what is happening now and less on what has taken place, it becomes easier for the brain to stay focused and in control. This includes avoiding problems relating to substance abuse, eating disorders, anxiety-related issues, and many other ongoing issues. Working with a better plan for mental health can make a real impact in one's life.

Being capable of staying mindful is a necessity for living that all people should follow. Those who are mindful will have a clear idea of what they want to get out of their lives. They will know that there are many good things in life worth looking forward to.

What People Can Do to Be Mindful

There are many good things that people can do when aiming to be mindful and in control of their lives. These points are vital for keeping anyone's mind under control and likely to stay positive and in check:

1. Start by focusing on certain natural breathing techniques.

Much of being mindful entails meditation. Natural breathing and concentration are vital to mindfulness. Part of this includes focusing on a present value or object. The goal is to allow for those feelings to stay comfortable. The key point is to feel comfortable and to be in a steady and comfortable place when practicing mindfulness. By understanding what one can do over time, it becomes easier for a person to feel positive and under control in one's life.

2. Notice how body sensations move along.

Many sensations might come about during the natural breathing process. Anything that is felt needs to be accepted for what it is. This includes recognizing any changes that have happened in the body and how the body is feeling relaxed.

3. Observe how emotions flow.

The interesting thing about emotions is that they are produced in many forms. Sometimes they might come out of the blue when certain events happen. The best way for a person to be mindful is to watch for how those emotions flow and how they are produced. Knowing what to expect from the past is important to recognize.

4. Stay concentrated on the emotions being felt at a given time.

The emotions one is experiencing at a certain moment should be considered. When a person is fully aware of what is happening, it becomes easier for people to feel positive and at ease with their minds.

Thinking about other emotions might only do more to hurt one's life. It is imperative for a person to look at where one's life is going and what changes might be coming about within it. Having an idea of what is happening in one's life is a necessity for going far and keeping that life in check without problems getting in the way of one's mindset.

5. Anyone who practices mindfulness must be persistent.

It takes a while for people to relax enough to be mindful. The key part of mindfulness is to stay the course and to keep working toward being emotionally invested in one's feelings. Practice always makes perfect when it comes to recognizing how one's feelings work and what can be experienced out of them at a time.

How Long Does It Take to Become Mindful?

Everyone responds to the process of being mindful in many ways. Some people will respond quickly, but others might have to practice this for a while. Sometimes it takes about 20 to 40 minutes in a single session to start focusing on what one can do to change one's life for the better. Regular mindfulness sessions help people to start thinking about what they can do with their lives. Practicing every day helps people decide what they can do to be strong and positive with whatever it is they want to do.

People should practice mindfulness at the same time each day. Working on mindfulness in the morning helps people to organize their thoughts so they can feel better every day. People can also work on it in the evening so the thoughts and feelings they picked up during the day can be arranged, thus giving a person a fuller meaning over everything that took place that day.

What About Single-Tasking?

People are occupied with many things in their lives that they feel that engaging in just one task at a time is going to keep them from being productive or active in whatever they are doing. However, single-tasking might be a necessity when all is considered.

Those who engage in single-tasking will focus on just one action while keeping one's full attention toward it. In this situation, a person will think less about what might happen and what is worthwhile and positive in one's life. People who concentrate on one thing at a time will have an opportunity for thinking about what one can do in life and how certain actions might cultivate a positive feeling of change.

The best part of single-tasking is that it allows a person to stay concentrated and ready to think about just one thing at a time. Knowing what one is getting into in a brief moment helps with understanding what should be done to change one's life for the better.

How to Organize Those Tasks

The single tasks that a person might engage in should be planned. It is through deciding which tasks are important. To make that life worthwhile, the tasks in question need to be organized. Several things can be done when trying to arrange tasks carefully. These points must work to help people see what they can do to grow as people and thrive:

1. Take a look at the things that have to be done in a day. Organize them in a list.

2. Look at how valuable each task is. Are there certain tasks that are more important than others?

Important tasks, in this case, might be things like a home maintenance task that needs to be resolved soon before damages can occur. Maybe there's a test at school that is worth more of one's grade than something else. There are also times when a task at work might have to be finished sooner than others.

3. Decide the weight of each task and then organize them based on what is important. Whatever absolutely has to be done first should be placed at the top.

4. Go through each of the items after organizing them. Decide what can be done to finish all the tasks.

Sometimes the tasks have to be reorganized based on how well they can be managed. A good rule of thumb is to keep the similar tasks organized together. Planning a smart list helps anyone with getting a clear idea of what can be done during the day.

Being mindful is a part of life that all people need to recognize regarding their emotional intelligence. Those who are mindful will be capable of keeping their mental functions under control without worrying. This is vital for having a positive life as it becomes easier for a person to feel confident and in control of one's life.

Chapter 17 – Social Awareness

The first two parts of emotional intelligence were about the self and understanding how one's mind can be regulated. The next two parts focus on understanding the opinions of other people.

Social awareness is understanding and responding to the demands that people have.

Cultures and organizations are unique. Everyone has their own set of values and interests that make them who they are. Those who are aware of the cultures in an area will be interested in what might be happening in any situation.

There are many positives that happen when a person is socially aware. A high EQ person will notice it is easy to move forward and be stronger with whatever it is one wishes to do with others. That person will get along with others because they understand what is happening in a society.

Three Vital Points

There are three critical aspects of social awareness that all people must know. These three considerations are critical to one's success in handling a better and more proficient life:

1. Empathy

Social awareness involves understanding the concerns that another person has. It is vital for people to feel empathy toward others as it is a sign of appreciation toward another and a desire to help. Empathy is being confident in others without being judgmental. More importantly, it is about understanding the concerns and needs that people have and how to accommodate them.

2. Organizational Awareness

The roles of individuals and how they manage certain tasks require organization. Organization is needed to help people do more and get the most out of the tasks they are trying to complete. An emotionally intelligent person will fully understand that there are needs that people have and that they can help.

3. Service

There will always be a need to serve people and to provide them with the help they need. This includes service in the form of helping people to find things in a store, have tasks done in their homes or offices and so forth. Social awareness is understanding what can be done to help people. Working with a plan for social awareness is vital to one's success in life. Social awareness is about helping people and seeing that their emotions and needs are being satisfied in the best manner possible.

The important thing about working on social awareness is to see that there are no issues coming about when trying to speak to people and to care for them. Social awareness is all about knowing that people have certain emotions and they must be considered.

Trust Is Critical

The most important part of social awareness is that developing this form of awareness helps a person to show one's value and understanding of how other people operate. It is through social awareness that a person can establish a sense of trust. When a person responds to the needs of others they will establish trust.

Understanding and comprehension are vital aspects of social awareness that have to be utilized. Anyone who knows what can be done to develop a better and more proficient life will be confident.

Accepting Opinions

Everyone has their own values in their lives. Some people have attitudes where they might hold radically different political viewpoints. Others might have their own hobbies or desires that are very different from what others have. Whatever the case may be, a socially aware person will always acknowledge that people have certain attitudes. This includes knowing that people are confident about who they are or what they believe in.

The more important aspect of working with people who have different views is that it helps to show a sense of acceptance and respect. Those who are willing to show a sense of positivity in life and a desire to acknowledge the values of others will go further and be appreciated more than other people in any situation.

People who want to get more out of their relationships have to be ready to handle the things they enter into in their lives. Every situation is unique and different. An emotionally intelligent person must recognize that all people have their own attitudes and values that they can live by. After understanding this, it becomes easier for someone to move forward in life.

Building Social Awareness

There are many good points that can be considered when aiming to develop social awareness.

1. Greet people using their names.

The first thing to do is to address people by their names if possible. A person can also be referred to as Sir or Madam. The point is to show that one understands a person's presence and that it is perfectly fine to get into communication with someone.

2. Pay attention to what people are saying.

Active listening is vital to anyone's success. It is through active listening that a person will understand the needs of others and will be ready to take action and contact people based on those concerns they might have.

3. Notice what happens when people respond to certain stimuli.

The responses that people make can vary. Some people might be surprised when they hear a greeting. Others might be happy or upset depending on what they find. Whatever the case is, the stimuli being produced should be explored. This ensures that nothing wrong could happen in any situation.

4. Notice what other people are saying to each other.

This next step does not involve eavesdropping on conversations. Rather, it is recognizing the emotions and feelings of people. A discussion can be talking about the concerns that people have and what they are thinking at a moment. It is through understanding the emotions that a person can become socially aware of what's happening at any given time.

5. Be willing to live in the moment.

Living in the moment is not always easy for people to do. It is through this that people can accept others for what might come along in life. People who are willing to live in the moment and get something out of it will surely be appreciated.

6. Be aware of the culture in an environment.

Every environment has its own rules for living. Some places might be formal and might require people to be on their best behavior. Others are environments where people are free to be themselves without having to follow strict rules.

Socially aware people understand that the cultures that they encounter are unique and special in various ways. They have to recognize what makes these cultures different and how they can be valuable and essential to one's life. Having some control over how these cultures are to be experienced can be vital for having a stronger and more productive life.

7. Accept that there is a diverse array of things that will come about in a zone.

Emotional intelligence is often about understanding that everyone is unique. For instance, there might be a large baseball stadium filled with fans cheering. The variety of fans in the venue would be rather different. Some people have different political values. Others might have certain religious standards to follow or dietary rules. In other words, even the largest grouping of people who have a shared interest will include an immense amount of diversity.

All people are unique in their own ways. One way to build emotional intelligence is to take a look at individual people and see what makes them different, unique, and special. By doing this, it becomes easier for someone to get along with others and to realize that there are many people out there who have attitudes and values that make them different.

Social awareness must be explored when finding a way to be stronger around people and capable of interacting with them well. It is through social awareness that it is easier for a person to communicate with others and to be stronger in the ways of contacting people. This is an aspect of emotional intelligence that cannot be ignored.

Chapter 18 – Managing Relationships the Right Way

High EQ people know that relationships are essential to their lives. They know that to get along with others, they have to discover what they can do to keep their relationships strong.

Relationship management is being able to handle others and to get along with them. High EQ people know what they have to do when getting in touch with people. They understand that there are many types of people who are different in many ways.

More importantly, relationship management is about inspiring and influencing people. This includes knowing how to manage the conflicts that might occur in life. Being able to get through the troubling conflicts and hassles that people encounter in their lives is a must.

Emotional intelligence is knowing how people can work with each other and how they can respond to different situations that happen in a relationship. It is through a strong relationship that people can interact with each other and feel better about what their lives.

There is no reason why people who are very different from one another cannot be good friends and do well in the same workplace. Having the ability to understand one another and how they respond to different things are critical to their success. People who do not know much about each other will struggle to go anywhere and be successful.

The Four Big Keys

Relationship management is dictated by four vital points in life. Each of these factors must be explored in detail to give a better idea of what to expect in a situation:

1. Decisions

Relationship management is often based on decisions. People have to make the right decisions in their lives based on all the things that are going to happen in the workplace or at home.

A high EQ person will know how to make decisions and find solutions that everyone in an environment will be comfortable with.

2. Interactions

The best interactions in relationship management involve people coaching others to success and helping them to find agreement or compromise. In other cases, such interactions will involve communicating well in a written form, when face-to-face or any other format. Whatever the case might be, the right interactions must be followed to let all people feel better about what they are doing.

3. Outcomes

Relationship management relies on outcomes. It is through coaching and educating people that the right outcomes can be accomplished.

4. The Needs of People

Every person in a group has their own needs. A high EQ person will understand that each person in an environment has distinct needs and requirements that are different from one another. Sometimes those needs are dictated by the personal demands that people have or even a shared goal at a business site. The needs are always going to change and evolve based on what people can do and how well they might interact with one another.

Each of these four keys is vital for relationship management. Planning a good relationship is a necessity for a healthy life, but there are many additional considerations that have to be explored when finding solutions that one can follow and work with.

Making Decisions

The aspects of managing relationships for one's emotional intelligence are diverse. To start, it helps to look at how decisions can be made. Businesses will make many decisions about what they want to do. They will do anything to get that advantage over the competition.

A high EQ person will know that decisions can do many things to help a business thrive. There are many things that can be done when making decisions to boost the business environment and make it stronger:

1. Look at the requirements that people have in their lives. What do they want to get out of the workplace?

2. Decide on what means can be utilized to achieve those needs. Aim to follow points as close to the original needs as possible.

3. Address the anxieties that people have. Let them know what can be done to neutralize those problems.

4. Plan a line of action for getting people together and feeling confident about something.

The efforts that go into planning a good relationship are often based on the decisions that people make. By developing one's emotional intelligence through making the right choices and planning, it becomes easier for a group to grow and thrive.

How to Influence People

The next point about relationship management involves knowing how to influence others and make them feel better about what is happening in a situation. It takes a person with a strong level of emotional intelligence to influence people and make them feel happy about what they are doing in their lives.

People who are emotionally bright will know how to influence others. The following steps may be used in a place to influence people and make them see things in a certain light:

1. Understand the motivations and needs that people have. People might feel strong desires to get along with others.

2. Be aware of what a person might feel when something happens. Look at what causes people to feel encouraged and ready to do things.

3. Talk with people based on the desires or feelings they have. Show a sense of empathy and appreciation for what those people are doing.

4. Discuss plans for what can be done and how well certain ideas might work to their benefit. Focus on what makes something worthwhile to a single person or a group of people. It is the target's feelings and values that are important, not what the person leading might feel.

People will start working toward doing something positive and productive with their lives if they know that there are good things to find in the things that they do.

Be an Inspiration

Everyone seeks a good inspiration in their lives. They want to be influenced by people who know what they can do to make themselves stand out and be intriguing to others. It is through the work that people provide that they can be great inspirations.

Emotional intelligence can be utilized to inspire a team and make it move forward. Here are a few of the things to do:

1. Be inclusive of everyone in a situation.

All people should be allowed to have a say in what might happen in a situation. This includes letting everyone share their values on what they feel is right for them and how they can change things in an environment for the better. People will feel inspired when they know they are playing a part in the success of a whole. The appreciation that someone will feel is often rewarding enough.

2. Suggest great paths for people to follow.

Everyone can work with appealing paths that are dynamic and unique in many forms. People might stick with certain paths where they are likely to go forward in their beliefs and attitudes.

3. Be willing to establish relationships with even those who have opposite viewpoints.

People are inspired when they see that their leaders are able to get along with others. Such relationships are a sign of peace among people. They prove that while some might have different attitudes and values, they can get along well and respect the differences that each other have.

People might be inspired when they notice that everyone in a relationship is supported. It is through this extra help that people will notice there is nothing to be worried about when trying to run an operation.

4. Stay positive even when things are tough.

Emotionally intelligent people know to look for the positive things in their lives. They don't dwell on the negative things in their lives. When people are positive and comfortable, they will feel excited about what can happen next. They aren't fearful about what could come about in a situation.

All of these points for inspiring people can make a difference in any working environment. People must see what they can get out of their inspirations when going forward and getting something extra out of life.

Coaching Pointers

Coaching is like leading people. It is through coaching that a person can establish powerful relationships where all people involved can agree with one another and recognize their strengths. Several things should be done when coaching others:

1. Have a clear vision.

Emotionally intelligent people are always certain about what they want to do and what they want to be done. Those people will instead think more about how they are helping others and getting people to feel positive.

Have a vision or series of objectives to live by and should be things that will positively influence everyone in an environment. Anything that offers extra support to people is always worth looking into for one's success and advancement.

2. Be clear and certain about what will be done.

People who are not familiar with what they can do to help people and not certain of what to do will be less likely to thrive and succeed.

A successful coach is someone who knows what can be done in any situation. This includes working with a plan to address the needs and concerns that people have. Knowing how to manage these problems and get more out of one's life is vital for success and for going forward in life.

3. Decide what the roles for people might be.

Every person in a group has their own strengths. It is through effective coaching that people are able to determine what is right for everyone to work with. The roles being used in a situation should be planned accordingly based on what might be right and how well things can work in any environment.

An emotionally intelligent coach will look at the things people can do in a situation. This includes knowing how well people can handle the things they want to say and share.

4. Never be hard on other people.

It is easy for someone to be rough and difficult when coaching. There have long been stories about coaches who have been hard to be around and are in some cases unorthodox or tough. They are often heralded by some as people who get results and command respect.

That does not mean that every coach will be successful using a harsh method. It takes effort and care to be around people and to support them. The best thing to do when coaching people is to be encouraging and to understand that every person has a unique learning style. It often takes longer for certain people to adapt to changes and rules and some people might adapt to them quickly. Being able to have some restraint and control over one's life and how it is managed can make a world of difference provided it is managed well.

5. Allow for a bit of leeway.

One error that people make when they coach others is that they might demand more than is necessary. This problem makes it a challenge for people to be comfortable.

Coaches should allow people to have a bit of leeway. That is, a person should be allowed to make mistakes on occasion or to veer off of a guided path. People should be given the right to be themselves while being corrected on occasion. This allows people to naturally ease their way into the behaviors that are wanted. Having this work in one's life can be essential for doing something more with one's emotions and getting them run perfectly.

Allow for Levity

People take things too seriously sometimes. It only takes a few moments for a person to get angry and struggle with a task. Even the serious things that people think about can get to be too difficult to manage. One positive thing to do to build one's EQ is to allow for a bit of humor. One of the greatest problems people have in society is that they are often too serious. Sometimes people are going to be angry over just the slightest things. Sometimes a person will get frustrated quickly and then become angry.

A high EQ person will know how to let people laugh and relax for a bit. There is always a brighter or lighter side to everything. Thinking about the negative things all the time will just cause a person to feel gloomy and unhappy with the tasks at hand.

Humor will relieve stress in anyone. Humor keeps a person's burden from being too intense. More importantly, it allows people to get a bit of perspective on what is happening in life. Those who are far too serious and tight about their lives will not enjoy themselves much because they are too busy thinking about all the negative things.

It never hurts to tell a joke or point out something amusing about a situation. Those who do this will not become worried or frustrated. More importantly, those people will be seen as positive and easier to trust. Those people have the best intentions of a business or other group in mind.

Being humorous reduces the brain's worries. It is very easy for people to make poor decisions when they are frustrated or dealing with lots of emotional turmoil. Those who are willing to rest and think about things will not be likely to feel frustrated or worried about what is going on in one's life.

Best of all, levity ensures that people in a relationship are not going to be critical of one another. Having a bit of lightheartedness in life can keep people relaxed.

People don't even need to be overly creative in their humor to enjoy what they are trying to do. All it takes is for someone to just think about something good to say or do when expressing humor. This, in turn, produces a comfortable feeling that all people can enjoy having in their lives.

Seeing a Perspective on Conflicts

The odds are there will be conflicts in the workplace or another environment. There is no way that people are going to agree on every single thing they come across. There might be disputes over what should be done in an environment. Such arguments can be about how to lead people or how to correct problems that occur or develop.

The last thing that people should do is develop problems that will persist and become difficult for anyone to handle. Conflicts have to be managed to keep a relationship from being a burden.

An emotionally intelligent thing to do to keep a relationship running right is to keep conflicts from being worse than necessary. There are many things that can be done to control a conflict:

1. Pick the right battles.

When trying to manage a dispute, it is important to look at what caused people to feel certain ways. Is a dispute going along for no real reason? Maybe there is something that might not be worth the time to handle. For instance, an issue where one person uses a parking space in a business lot versus another is not something all that important to resolve. The only battles that should be handled are the ones that directly influence how people are going to behave and how it affects their work.

2. Be respectful of the opinions that someone else has.

No one should be chastised for believing in something different from everyone else. Having a strong opinion to resolve a conflict with can make a world of difference if handled correctly.

3. Empathize with the other views that people hold.

Every viewpoint exists for a reason. People need to respect the views and opinions of others. Failing to do this would defeat the purpose of emotional intelligence as it does not recognize what makes people act in certain ways.

4. Recognize a need to target the issue directly.

One of the reasons why disputes go on longer than needed is because people do not think about what is the cause of an argument. People often become angry to the point where they cannot tolerate dissent or other disagreements any further.

A high EQ person will be ready to handle a problem right away and to address the concern before it becomes worse. Knowing how to get past such a problem is vital to the success of any relationship.

5. Find an in-between point that the two sides will appreciate.

It is often impossible for people to see each side of an argument. Some people might refuse to accept one side by calling it irrational or impossible to work with. Others would feel that an argument is too much of a burden or challenge to solve.

Fortunately, people can resolve issues by finding strong in-between points. This includes finding solutions that meet the needs of both sides. This often takes extensive negotiations at times, but the goal is to get both sides to feel comfortable with what they are doing and trying to achieve. Getting to that agreement is vital, but it is even more important for people to avoid getting into heavy disputes with each other after that. Most of these problematic disputes come from people disagreeing with one another.

6. Be ready to forgive and forget.

When people dwell upon conflicts for too long, it becomes easy for them to blame each other for problems and to get into fights. This, in turn, causes people to be isolated from one another. They feel that they can no longer work with one another without getting into further disputes or arguments.

Being able to forgive and forget a dispute is always important. As a problem can resolve, the two sides should recognize that they had their own differences but they can still try to get along. This allows people to stay together and to keep working toward the same goal.

The amount of time it takes to get one of these conflicts resolved will vary based on the issues at hand and what people are trying to accomplish by fixing a problem. Sometimes a conflict might be too complicated. In other cases, that conflict might be easy to handle if people think a little more about where they are going with it. Knowing what to get out of a conflict and how to stop the issue from becoming worse is vital to one's success.

Chapter 19 – The Motivational Aspects of Emotional Intelligence

One part of emotional intelligence that is vital for a great relationship is to understand how people are motivated. It is through motivation that people are able to get along with each other and support the needs that one another might have.

Motivation focuses on how to get the self and others to achieve and do more with their lives. The point places an emphasis on getting everyone in a situation to grow and thrive. It takes effort for people to feel committed and ready to achieve goals together. When people are motivated, they know that there is something on the horizon for them to look forward to.

Naturally, not everyone can be motivated easily. A low EQ person might not feel all that much motivation. A high EQ person will operate differently. They will feel motivated and know what can be done. They will be stronger and happier with their life without struggling with what one wants to do.

Four Keys of Motivation (and How to Attain Them)

Being motivated takes effort. It is understandable as to why some people might not feel motivated. Maybe a person is too fatigued and might not have a desire to get out and do things. Perhaps someone is too afraid of what might happen when starting a certain task.

There are four aspects of motivation that directly influence what someone can expect to get out of being motivated and in control of one's life:

1. A person will have a personal drive to get out there and move ahead.

A personal drive to get out and do things is a necessity for all to have in their lives. Sometimes the personal drive might be to achieve a goal. The drive can include trying to reach specific standards or even to improve upon the standards that someone has met in the past. A high EQ person will know what one's drive might be and can also figure out the drives that others have, thus making it easier for them to influence others.

To get a good drive, it helps to look at one's experiences in life. What is causing one's emotional state to change and move forward? What makes a person want to go far and do more with life? By looking at these parts of one's drive, it becomes easier to grow as a person.

2. Motivated people are committed to what they want to do.

Low EQ people do not a commitment to do things. They might not assume that what they are doing is all that important. High EQ people are different; they know that they have goals that they really want to achieve.

To become committed, a person must look at the goals they have. What will happen when a goal is met? Will it result in a better and more productive life? By recognizing the positive aspects of what one can do, it becomes easier for that person to be committed and ready to handle whatever happens.

3. People who are motivated are ready to get anything done.

Readiness is different from motivation, but there is a link between the two. When a person is motivated, they will feel a need to do something. When that individual is ready, it means the motivation will be acted upon as soon as possible. When a person is ready to do things, it becomes easier to go far and evolve.

To become ready, it is important to understand what one requires to get a job done. Sometimes the requirements for finishing a task include having the right resources. In other cases, a sense of knowledge is important. No matter what the requirements for a task might be, it is vital for people in any situation to know what they need to do their tasks and to finish them the right way.

4. Optimism is a necessity for motivation.

People who are motivated will feel optimistic about what can happen. They will not fear the things that are coming along in their lives. Instead, they will do what they can to grow and become stronger. When a person has a sense of optimism, they will do better with life. That person is going to think about the good things in life and how they will produce a better result. Having a sense of positivity will make all the difference when aiming to get someone to go along with life and feel better about it.

To attain a sense of optimism, it helps to look at the negative things that one might perceive. Sometimes those negatives are unrealistic or are not likely to happen. These problems should be discounted if possible so they will not make a negative impact on what someone is doing at the moment.

How to Be a Better Motivator

The challenges associated with trying to motivate people are often difficult. People are worried about what they can get out of others when trying to motivate them. Several things must be used when trying to motivate people and make them feel great about a situation:

1. Discover what causes people to have strong drives.

A high-EQ individual will understand that getting along with people is easy when their desires are known. The needs that people have and their hopes for the future should be considered when figuring out what the right thing to do is.

2. Help people to keep on learning.

Emotionally intelligent people know that there is no way to be perfect. The effort to get out there and become a stronger individual from a mental perspective is a never-ending effort.

It is a necessity for people to keep learning new things. Those who can learn well will be more successful and likely to do more with whatever they want to do.

3. Explain the benefits of what is happening to others.

People are more likely to feel motivated when they understand there are benefits to whatever it is they are being told to do. It becomes easier for people to feel encouraged to keep working and to get more out of the tasks they have to complete.

4. Show a desire to be on someone's side.

Anything can happen when trying to motivate people. This includes working to show that someone is positive and confident.

Motivation is easy when people are encouraged and are helped to be better and stronger.

Chapter 20 – Building Empathy

Although anyone can work hard toward figuring out one's own emotions and the emotions of other people, it is even more important to relate to those outside emotions. No one likes a person who is impersonal or not willing to address certain concerns or values with other people. When a person can build empathy, it becomes easier for them to relate to others.

Everyone appreciates someone who can show that they understand the emotions and feelings that others have. There is always a good reason why a person is behaving in a certain way.

It is through empathy that a person is able to connect with others and share certain attitudes or ideas with others. Empathy is thinking about the emotions that another person has. The best way to describe this is that a person is putting himself or herself in someone else's shoes.

The concept of empathy is critical to one's emotional intelligence. It is through empathy that a person can show that he or she understands what someone is thinking or feeling. Empathy helps people to do many things in particular:

- People who have empathy will understand the thoughts that someone else has. Empathy produces better relationships between people. Everyone in a relationship will trust one.

- People will want to share information with one another when they show empathy. They can share things with others and be ready to express their feelings.

- The workplace will be easier to manage when everyone shows empathy. They will become more productive and capable of working with each other.

People can build upon their EQ levels by becoming more empathetic. This is all about knowing what people are thinking so it becomes easier to interact with others.

Abandon Personal Viewpoints

The first thing a person can do to build one's sense of empathy is to discard previously assumed views, stereotypes, and biases. For example, Dave might be surprised that his co-worker Mike is drinking his coffee really fast. Dave might feel that Mike is worried and that he is so agitated that he is drinking coffee faster than usual. Maybe Dave might think that Mike is angry or frustrated with someone, possibly him.

When Dave asks Mike why he is so frustrated, he will suddenly notice that Mike is not angry or upset. He is simply drinking his coffee faster because he doesn't want it to get cold.

The best thing that Dave can do to build upon his EQ is to avoid assuming that something is happening for whatever reason. Being willing to ask questions and to think about all the circumstances surrounding something is vital to one's EQ.

Personal preconceptions make it harder for people to get along with others. Showing empathy for other views and to never assume things based on one's beliefs is critical for developing a stronger relationship with others.

Acknowledge the Other Emotion

Empathy requires recognizing the emotion that a person is expressing. In the example, Dave can state that he sees why Mike is doing something in some way. He knows that Mike is not behaving out of anger but out of another feeling.

Even when one does not agree with the other perspective, the emotion should be confirmed and supported. By acknowledging another emotion, it becomes easier for people to recognize what others might be feeling. It is through this that people can relate to each other.

A person who wants to acknowledge an emotion can do so by engaging with that person and doing one of many things:

- That person might talk briefly about the emotion someone is feeling.

- A discussion on what can be done to manage one's life can take place.

- A talk on how the emotion came about is always welcome. People might feel better about what is happening in their lives if they talk about what they are going through.

Anything that can be done to recognize emotions and feelings is always worthwhile. The key is to keep oneself from sounding or appearing distant from another person.

Review Attitudes

Empathy can be handled when the attitudes that people have toward one another are analyzed. People have their own inspirations for why they want to do things in certain ways:

- Some people simply want to get ahead and be more successful.

- Others want to be right and show that they are smarter than anyone else.

- Many people want to be accepting of each other. They are trying to find answers to how many people with different attitudes can communicate with one another.

A person who wants to build empathy must recognize that everyone's attitudes are different. The best thing to do is to look at what inspires individuals in the workplace or in one's life to act in certain ways. Getting an idea of what makes people act in certain ways gives people extra control over their lives.

It is through understanding that it becomes easier for someone to become empathetic and ready to accept what others are feeling.

Listening Is Key

People take listening for granted. They might just hear certain things without thinking about what they mean or what value those points have. When someone listens, it becomes easier for them to want to do things with someone else.

Those who listen closely to other people will be likely to develop empathy. This part of EQ helps people to understand that there are many things that someone is saying and that there are many reasons why someone has certain feelings or attitudes.

The most important part of listening is listening to an entire message without any interruptions. People who pay attention to an entire message will have a sense of understanding for what someone is trying to say. This includes the following:

- Listen to the words being used. Some words might be stronger than others or might carry a greater weight.

- Review the tone and speed of how things are being said.

- Pay attention to anything someone says regardless of who the target audience is. Sometimes a person talks to people in one way and then talks to other people in a different manner. Such changes may dictate what comes about when listening to others.

How to Listen

To listen properly, a person needs to know how to manage the conversation. There are four vital keys that must be followed when trying to listen to someone and figure out what that person has to say.

1. Listening with the Ears

The first key is listening to what someone is saying. Listening with the ears is the most basic. This goes beyond just paying attention to the things that someone is saying. Several added points must be put into play when listening with one's ears:

- The things that are being said have some kind of meaning to them.

- The vocabulary involved should be checked too. Some words might be more intense than others.

- The tone being used should be noticed. The tone might be stern or light. A person might be lighthearted or joking about something, but in other cases, that person might be serious.

- The speed at which someone says something is important to notice. When a person talks fast, it becomes clear that the person is trying to rush a conversation. Those who talk slowly might be confused, uncertain, or otherwise worried about what is happening.

2. Listening with the Eyes

The nonverbal communication that someone uses when speaking is important. Sometimes the words that a person says do not reflect what they are feeling. Watching for nonverbal cues allows a person to really understand what someone is feeling. That other person will feel appreciated. It is a sign that the listener cares.

3. Listening to One's Heart

It is through a person's heart that true feelings and attitudes can come alive and become easier to notice. A person should listen to someone's heart to get a clear idea of what that person is thinking and feeling at the given moment.

So, what does it mean to listen to a person's heart? Listening to someone's heart is paying attention to what someone might be feeling or thinking. When a person's heart is considered, it becomes easier to understand why someone is feeling something or if that person has an attitude that is clearly removed from what is in reality. There is a chance that someone might be afraid of things in life and would not be fully certain as to what can go on and change in life.

Listening to the heart is about knowing what someone is feeling. There are many ways how a person's heart can be considered:

- Figure out the gut feeling that someone holds. These feelings include assumptions that keep a person from feeling confident or relaxed with a certain situation.

- Look at what someone is fixated on. Sometimes a person's heart might be far off from one's mind.

- Stop thinking about rational considerations. There are often times when a person is not thinking rationally; avoiding those points when listening to someone helps to see how that person's attitudes are changing and what might be causing that person to feel a certain way.

- Review the flow of ideas. This includes seeing how well thoughts connect with each other.

The heart often acts on a different wavelength from the brain. Knowing what it takes to manage the heart and to stay comfortable can make a true difference if one listens to whatever is happening at a time.

4. Listening Based on Instincts

Every person has instincts. Some people notice things sooner than others. A plan for listening should entail looking at when something is wrong in one's words. Instincts to follow include these points:

- Is a person sounding uncertain about their words?

- Are there any things happening right now that might be causing someone to speak in a certain fashion?

- Are there things that a person is trying to avoid?

The instincts one has might not always be correct. A person should avoid being overly dependent on instincts.

Active Listening

People who have empathy do more than just pay attention to the things that someone might say. An empathetic person also knows that there is a deeper meaning in whatever someone is saying. It becomes easier for that person to identify and gauge the emotions that someone has. More importantly, the empathetic person will know that there is a method to whatever someone is feeling.

Active listening is a part of EQ that allows a person not only to hear the words but also recognizes the overall message being conveyed.

Active listening is about keeping the focus on the words being said without being distracted. The key is to avoid things like trying to form a response or argument to whatever is being said. A person must also avoid getting bored or otherwise start to focus on things outside of the conversation.

The best way to describe this part of empathy is that it is about having the other person in a conversation feel appreciated. The biggest problem people have when trying to communicate is that they often feel that they aren't being paid attention to. They feel as though their words are going nowhere because the audience in question does not have interest in whatever is being said.

With the right form of empathy and enough active listening to work, it becomes easier for someone to feel appreciated. A person will notice that he or she is being listened to because the feelings in whatever is being said are being recognized. This can go a long way in any relationship.

Of course, active listening entails more than just giving a simple nod of the head or saying something like "yeah" or "yes" on occasion when listening to someone. Rather, active listening is about knowing there is a reason why someone says things. It is an acknowledgment not so much on the topic or statement but rather on what someone feels or the hidden messages that are being conveyed.

Multiple steps must be used to make active listening work.

1. First, a person has to pay attention to whatever is being said at all times.

Whoever is speaking must get all the attention in a room. The speaker must be observed directly. Direct eye contact shows a sense of respect but also gives the listener a better idea of what someone is thinking based on how the eyes are changing and moving.

Environmental factors have to be avoided or at least ignored at this point. Such factors include issues like conversations between other people, others moving around, or different items on a table.

The nonverbal cues should be noticed as well. These cues include everything from the arms changing position to the eyes looking a little different or possibly fatigued from something. Any nonverbal cues that are expressed might show some hidden feeling that a person has.

2. Give acknowledgments on occasion that attention is being heeded.

Although it is true that just nodding or saying that one is paying attention is not the only thing that should be done. Body language can be used in many forms to show that attention is being heeded.

Nodding and smiling is good, but it helps to change one's facial expressions based on any changes in the dialog. The listener's posture should be open and accepting as well. A conversation should not be verbally interrupted for more than half a second or so. Just letting out a brief note of acknowledgment is good enough.

3. Offer feedback on what is being said.

Feedback should be provided to a person about whatever is going on in a situation. Feedback can be anything relating to what is being said. The most common type of feedback is acknowledging an emotion or confirming the accuracy of what is being said.

There are many ways feedback can be given to a speaker:

- Say something that reflects upon whatever is being said. This could entail a statement like "What I am hearing is" or "So what you want to say" or anything else. The response here should not be a summary of what is being said but rather a recognition of whatever might be coming along in a certain situation.

- Questions about what was being said can be asked. Questions like "What do you mean by..." allows a person to confirm whatever is being stated. Planning good questions allows for a more reasonable approach.

- Brief summaries of what a person is saying can be offered provided they are not too lengthy. The summary is a simple statement showing that attention was paid to the speaker.

Don't just restate the same things a person said verbatim. Instead, use language that is unique to the situation.

4. Avoid judging people for what they are saying.

It is easy for people to be judged on what they are saying or doing. People like to pass judgments because they feel they are authentic points in their minds. They want things to skew toward their feelings.

When someone judges the things a person says, the conversation quickly takes a back seat. The main key to avoiding judgment is to let the other person in a conversation finish what he or she is saying before trying to say something else. When a person is interrupted, it becomes easy for misconceptions to be formed. More importantly, the speaker might feel unhappy with the listener because the speaker feels as though that person was not being paid proper attention.

There should not be any counter-arguments offered. Although it is easy to try and convince a person that someone is wrong, that is not going to help anyone to build empathy. This part of EQ only comes when a person is willing to hear someone else and figure out the meaning of whatever it is someone wants to say. Keeping counter judgments from happening is a must for paying attention to someone.

5. Be ready to respond in an appropriate fashion.

An active listener is supposed to be respectful. This includes being ready to respond to someone by recognizing what that person wants to convey. Active listening often entails being open and direct in a response. This can include being willing to show a sense of appreciation and recognition of whatever is being said.

Any responses should be respectful. A high EQ person will know that there is no need to judge a person over what they might be thinking at a time. Being ready to respond to a person in a respectful and generous manner will be appreciated.

Active listening makes the targeted person feel they are being listened to.

Be Willing to Ask Questions

The last point about building empathy for one's EQ is to ask questions. It helps to get a first-hand account of what someone is thinking.

For instance, Tina might ask Jennifer to talk about what is going on with her. Tina might notice that Jennifer feels reserved and quiet. Tina would have to ask Jennifer about her life and why she is feeling a certain way. When a person asks about one's emotions, it becomes easier for a person to think more about what someone is thinking or feeling.

However, this strategy is one that many people do not use when it comes to empathy. The fact is that while a high EQ person will have an easy time reading someone's feelings; it can be difficult for someone to get answers unless that person asks someone about them directly.

In the case above, Tina might say, "You don't seem as open as you usually are. What's going on?" Tina is saying this out of curiosity because she knows that her friend is acting differently from what she is usually like. Tina wants to show a sense of concern. She wants to see what the issue is and what she can do about it. By showing empathy, she is letting Jennifer know that she has an ally in whatever is happening.

This works best when a person's strategy for contacting someone is flexible. It is through a flexible plan for communication that it might be easier for a person to get in touch with someone.

The questions can be direct and straightforward, but they must also be asked with care and concern for someone. This includes seeing that the person who is being consulted is appreciated well and is not going to be judged or treated differently.

Some people might be afraid to ask questions. This is understandable as people often do not want to infringe upon the lives of others. They might be curious, but they also know that asking too many questions may not be appreciated. A high EQ individual will know that people are not going to be overly upset when they are being asked questions about various things. All a person has to do is start the conversation and politely ask about something of value. By doing so, that person will be more likely to get a better answer.

Types of Questions To Ask

A high EQ person will understand that there are many types of questions that can be asked in any situation. This section is about the questions that should be asked when trying to show empathy.

1. Open-Ended Questions

The best way to address a person when building empathy is to use open-ended questions. Open-ended questions come in many forms and suit the needs of various people. Some of the more popular open-ended questions that can be asked include the following:

- Questions that cause people to open up about what they are doing. Questions like "What were you doing to..." are always useful.

- Some questions focus on trying to get more detail or information on what someone is doing. A question like this may entail something like "What is happening with..."

- A person might want to find out what the issues or concerns a person might have, such as "What do you think about..."

The most important part about open-ended questions is that they allow for empathy to form as people are not likely to feel pressured.

2. Closed Questions

Closed questions are the opposite of open-ended questions. These do not do much to build empathy, but they can work in some cases.

For instance, a person might ask "I see that you're planning a vacation. I hope it's something exciting".

A person might ask a closed question. The question might be "When are you going on vacation?" or "How long will your vacation be." These are closed questions as each question has a very specific answer needed.

A high EQ person will know to use a closed question after an open one. Doing so the other way around only makes the conversation awkward and difficult.

A closed question works with the following points in mind:

- It can help to confirm an answer. A question like "If you do this, are you going to get a special reward?"

- Closed questions help to frame a point of interest. A closed question might include something like "How confident are you in..." or "Are you feeling good about..." among others that have very specific answers.

- Some questions are ideal for ending a conversation. These questions might include "Is this the best thing to do?" or "Are there any other ideas?"

The closed questions being used should not be confrontational.

3. Funnel Questions

Sometimes the questions being asked have to be whittled down. This means starting out in a general sense and then going down into a more specific setup. The questions used in this case are funnel questions.

Such questions are prominent among high EQ people. In such an instance, the questionnaire is going to start out broad and then specific.

- Start by talking about a broad event or issue. Ask about that point in general.

- Ask about something a little more specifically relating to the main subject.

- Go into as much detail as possible. Try to come up with multiple steps to get down to the heart of the matter.

For instance, Jeff is talking with Mike about a sporting event he went to. Jeff might start by asking, "I hear you were at a big sporting event the other day." After Mike tells him about the event, Jeff will then say "What was going on with the event?" Soon after, Jeff could ask, "Anything really fun happening?"

Maybe the questions would become more specific based on Mike's responses. Mike might say, "The concessions at the stadium are very good." Jeff would then say, "I love how creative they are. Anything really neat?"

By asking specific questions, Jeff would get more details from Mike about what happened. Mike will be eased into those specific questions. His mindset will have improved to where he will want to answer those questions and give Jeff a better idea of what was happening.

More importantly, Jeff understands that Mike doesn't want to be thrown into something that he might not be fully comfortable with. He instead wants to ask questions that Mike will be eased into without being forced to go into some intense specifics that might be a challenge to answer.

Funneling down the questions being asked makes the interview process more comfortable. It is through funneling that people will go from one extreme to the next without rushing things in the process.

4. Probing Questions

Probing questions are used when people want to get extra details on something being said or done. The best way to consider probing questions is to think about the six big points that everyone always talks about – who, what, when, where, why and how. Probing questions focus on the basics.

It helps to only ask probing questions when trying to clarify something being said.

When a person talks about something, the probing questions being utilized should be kept in check. Good probing questions are smart provided they are kept without causing pressure or stress over trying to give good answers.

The key is to be gentle when asking a probing question. Avoid asking anything that might be too intense or too personal. The odds are a person might not be ready to answer something deep or direct. It takes time for someone to get used to questioning and to feel better about whatever might be asked at a time.

5. Rhetorical Questions

Not all questions have to be direct. Rhetorical questions are good ones for people to ask. These are questions that allow people to ask something without necessarily soliciting a direct response.

A high EQ person will use rhetorical questions often. These are used because they are easy to pose and do not force a person into having to answer.

For instance, Jeff might try to ask Mike about the sporting event he went to. Jeff could say something like "Isn't that team doing well right now?" The question produces a good outcome that requires someone to share certain values.

There is a need to be respectful of people when trying to talk with them and engage in a meaningful conversation.

A Final Word About Empathy

The best relationships are the ones where people feel as though they are being cared for. No one wants to go through life alone; empathy helps people feel they matter and someone cares.

It is through empathy that people are capable of talking to each other and having a personal connection where everyone in a situation feels confident about what is going on. When the people who are being talked to feel comfortable, everyone will start to feel better about what is being discussed.

Asking questions helps to get an idea of what someone is thinking. Listening actively and knowing what a person has to say about something is always worthwhile too. The important thing is that people cannot assume that certain things are going to work in specific ways. People have to watch carefully and make sure they express a sense of empathy without being overwhelming. It is through empathy that people can get along.

Knowing how to build upon empathy makes a person easier to approach and more positive around others. Having this empathy makes a real difference when trying to reach others and help them see things in a certain way.

Chapter 21 – Conflict Management

It helps to look at how conflicts are to be managed. No one wants to enter into a conflict. Disputes make it harder for people to get along. Those who are emotionally intelligent know what they can do to keep those conflicts in check. It is through one's EQ that things can be done to keep a dispute or other concern in the workplace or elsewhere from becoming worse.

Why Conflicts Are Difficult

The reason why conflicts are difficult for many is that they trigger responses in the mind that make it harder for people to stay confident. Part of this comes from the classic concept of flight vs. fight.

A person who is passive and not willing to handle a conflict will go into flight and avoid the situation. This could make the issues at hand worse.

Someone who is aggressive and wants to dominate will enter into a fight. While they try to defuse the situation, the hostility and aggression might make the situation worse.

Those who do not have a high EQ will enter into the flight vs. fight situation. They will choose one side based on what they are thinking and will stick with it. A person might not be fully aware of what is causing a dispute. The hassles that come about might make the situation at hand harder to solve.

Managing Conflict

Several things can be done to keep a conflict under control and to prevent it from being a problem. More importantly, these points can stop a conflict altogether.

1. Make a series of factual statements addressing the problem at hand.

The first thing to do is to address the concern. There needs to be a sense of understanding when a conflict arises. Having some comprehension of what is going on is vital for helping people to resolve the dispute and to keep it from being a problem.

For instance, workplace manager Janet might notice there is a dispute in the workplace between Tom and Carl, two people who are trying to manage a business expansion project. The two men are arguing over how it will be completed. Tom might feel that the business needs to expand with more locations. Carl feels that the business should offer more services. The two have very different views and feel that each other's viewpoint will hurt the business in the long run.

Janet would have to get all the information about the situation at hand. She would ask Tom and Carl to explain their views. She needs to know why they are disagreeing with each other. By gathering all the facts, she has a clear idea of what the two men are thinking about. This gives her the control she needs over the conflict to plan a solution that might work.

2. Ask questions to the people.

It is imperative to ask questions to the people who are in the conflict. Ask them about their concerns and what they want to do with their objectives.

Janet would talk with Tom and Carl about the situation. Janet would ask Tom many questions: What makes you feel that it is best for the business to expand into many locations? Why would this work for the business? Where would the business go? She would then do the same with Carl: What types of services do you feel would work? How would they be handled throughout the entire workplace as it is?

3. Listen to what the people in the dispute have to say.

There is a chance that people in a dispute have certain opinions or feelings that need to be expressed. In Janet's case, she might notice that Carl is feeling confident about how well the business is laid out and what he wants to get out of it. He thinks that by expanding services, the business will have guaranteed ways to make revenue. Tom might tell her that the business needs to expand toward many places to reach a larger number of people.

Janet needs to listen to all sides of the dispute. She needs to see what is happening between the parties so she knows what to expect in a situation. By listening to both sides, she will understand what needs to be done to make a business grow and thrive.

4. Avoid passing judgment.

This mantra of emotional intelligence makes it ways into conflict resolution. Janet would need to think fairly of the two people in the argument and see that they have their own ideas. Janet should not think about anything that happened in the past with these two people. Rather, she should decide what is appropriate to her based on what she feels is right and sensible for the growth of a business.

5. Talk about a good outcome.

What is needed is an outcome that everyone will be comfortable with. This includes looking at the facts involved and figuring out what might be right for all people.

For this example, Janet would talk with the two about the expansion plans and think about everything from a realistic standpoint. This includes looking at how well people in the business have made plans. Knowing how to have a smart outcome is a necessity for getting a business to grow and succeed. The outcome may need to be a compromise. Janet would need to look at what can be done to get the people on both sides of the argument to agree.

6. Hold a full discussion.

The last part of managing a conflict is to hold a complete discussion where the two sides of the argument can get together to figure out what they should be doing. This includes establishing a series of rules.

Whatever choice Janet makes in the end, it will be based on her discussion with Carl and Tom about what they are doing. She will talk with each of them about their situations and plans while deciding what can be done to resolve certain issues.

These steps for managing a conflict are simple ones that must be followed for a business to become successful and to thrive. It is through conflict management that it becomes easier for people to correct themselves and to be stronger over time.

The most important part of this process is that it keeps a conflict from becoming worse. Many businesses and relationships struggle when disputes go on for too long. Those extended disputes can make it harder for people to get along with each other and to hear each other out.

Chapter 22 – Being a Catalyst For Change

Change is hard for everyone. No one likes change because it can be unpredictable. Change is vital in life for allowing anyone to feel better about certain things that are happening and to be able to adapt to whatever might come about in the future.

A person with a high emotional intelligence will be more likely than others to help support change. The goal is to not only encourage change but to also make people in the same environment feel that the change is useful and a necessity for everyone.

Why Do People Refuse Change?

It helps to understand why people aren't willing to change. There are many reasons people want things to stay the same.

1. A person might feel comfortable with one's situation.

A sense of complacency can settle in after a while. A man who gets up, has a toast for breakfast, takes the bus to work, gets back home after a bit of time, has a beer and watches television and then goes to sleep might be complacent with that routine. He knows that there are things coming about in his life each day that he can expect.

It might be difficult to adapt and adjust when something else comes up during that time frame. What if the bus isn't available? What if there's nothing good on television? Practically anything can disrupt that man's lifestyle. Still, people like often try to stay with the routines they are in because they know they can avoid problems. They want to keep on living in those ways so they will not be judged or rushed into situations that they do not want to be in.

   2. Something might be working already.

Another reason for people to resist change is that they might feel that change is not necessary. The things that are happening in a workplace or other environment might be just fine. For instance, a retail store location is getting better sales thanks to some of its promotions and new products. That location has higher sales right now than what it had last year or the year before.

People often refuse change at this point because they feel that whatever is working well should be left alone. After a while, there could be a chance for a change to take place. Maybe a business will stop growing as well as it has been because people are far too used to whatever is available.

   3. There's a sense of uncertainty with change.

Uncertainty comes when people are afraid of change and don't know what to expect. This is a point that makes it harder for people to take that next step.

A business might want to expand and grow to offer more services or locations. At the same time, that business might not be willing to make a change.

   4. People have biases over how things are going to work for them.

The biases that people hold are sometimes based on false opinions. They focus on the issues they have in their personal lives. For instance, people might think that certain outside factors that cause change are dangerous. They could assume that those factors are dangerous and are not going to help them in the least. Sometimes those biases will cloud people vision about the situations they might enter into. Those people will not understand that there is something positive to be had out of the work being produced and how well it can run. This makes knowing how to get a bias-corrected and fixed all the more important for people to explore.

These four points prove that people have their own reservations and worries about change. They don't know what would happen when change takes place. Sometimes they might be too content to go forward and make those changes.

By using one's emotional intelligence, it becomes easier for change to happen and become easier to manage.

How to Make Change Work

Being capable of inducing a change in the workplace is not always easy. It takes effort and a strong will to get people to see just how important change can be. Even those who have been fixated on a certain routine for a long time will find that it is not difficult to make changes when the right plans and efforts for work are put into play.

1. Be positive about the change.

Emotionally intelligent people are not afraid of what might happen. They have reviewed all the situations they are entering into and know that there is always going to be something great coming out of the work one puts in. Catalysts also know that it is not a problem to change things and to make a situation more positive.

An emotionally intelligent person must be ready to suggest positivity over anything that might be planned.

2. Be a visionary.

Visionary people are those who are not afraid to look forward. This includes looking into what might happen when a change takes place. People could see that by making the right changes, lives will be easier to lead and people will be happier with what they are doing. However, it is through one's visionary work that such changes can be promoted.

People should focus on being visionary by highlighting the great things that they can do with their lives. Knowing how to get people to feel confident and relaxed about what they are doing in their lives can make a real difference if managed well enough.

3. Express a likable quality.

Change catalysts need to show that the changes they want to support are ones that people can get behind. This includes being likable and friendly toward others. A sense of positivity and likeability is vital for making any kind of change work well. It is through being upbeat and confident that a person can grow and succeed. More importantly, people will be happy about changes when they see the positives.

An emotionally intelligent person will always think about the benefits that can come with certain actions. It is through that positive attitude that a person can go do more and be a better person for all to follow and support.

4. Be open to the change.

One problem that many have with change is that they don't always seem to be positive or worthwhile. Sometimes those changes might be difficult for people to comprehend. They might see issues in those changes and don't want to follow. But the reason for this might be because they don't understand all the points that come with it.

Take a look at an investment opportunity that might be posted online. People are often suspicious of these things. They don't know what makes an investment worthwhile or interesting. When a white paper or other document explaining everything is posted, it becomes easier for people to support something. They will see that an investment features many points relating to success.

Those who are open to change understand that people have various needs and worries. By handling the right changes over time, it becomes easier for people to grow and stay strong. Those people will do their best when they know there are lots of details for them to follow that can make a true difference in their plans and for how they will work.

5. Express a strategic plan.

Being a change catalyst requires establishing a good strategy. The strategy can be anything from a plan for expanding to a schedule for how concepts are to be developed. The details that go into the plan must be specific so people can feel better about supporting something being offered.

A strategic plan should be explored when trying to make emotional intelligence work. It is through this that people can convey a sense of understanding over the changes that will take place.

6. Acknowledge and review any biases people have.

Consider the biases that people hold. Everyone has some kind of bias. Some people have biases that are a little more intense than others. They might feel that there are lots of things that could hurt them and that they need to get away from those issues if they want to succeed. Some people feel that certain procedures will not work all that well. Others think that specific behaviors are not worthwhile and that they might hurt people who try to follow them.

There is a need to look at the biases that people have and to see what can be done to resolve those biases. Knowing how to target these biases and stop them from developing any further is a necessity for allowing a business to grow and stay strong.

The main point of the process is to help people see what makes changes useful while opening their eyes to seeing how they can benefit. This includes convincing them that there is nothing to worry about. Recognizing the emotions people have over change while supporting a plan will help those people to stay comfortable with whatever is being promoted.

Change is always good for people. It is what helps people to feel better about their lives and will help them to grow and evolve as strong citizens of society. An emotionally intelligent person will be more likely to convince people that the changes they need are right for them.

Chapter 23 – Establishing Collaboration

Collaboration is a vital part of work. Those who know how to work with others and not create any problems will feel better about the efforts they are putting in.

People in today's work environments are not as sure about their skills or talents as they used to be. In the past, people would feel confident and think that they can complete their tasks on their own. As times have changed, projects in the workplace have become harder to follow and use.

People have to work together and collaborate if they want to go far and stay ahead in their lives. It is through collaboration that people can combine all of their skills to do many things.

A good example of this can be seen on a professional ice hockey team. There is no realistic way one person could carry all the weight. An ice hockey team needs great forward who can score goals, defensemen who can move the puck across the ice, and a goaltender who can stop an opponent's shots. In other words, even someone as legendary and talented as Wayne Gretzky isn't going to do things on his own. He needs assistance to succeed.

Having a sense of collaboration is vital to success in the workplace too. All members in a workplace have certain skills and attributes that make them worthwhile and essential to the success of a business.

A high EQ person will do what it takes to produce a healthy environment where everyone in a workspace can work together and work to their best capabilities to grow and become better workers. It is through collaboration that people will feel positive and capable of going places in their lives. To make it all work, a good environment that is conducive to collaborative efforts has to be produced.

What Makes Collaboration Great?

Collaboration helps a business or other group to become stronger and likely to keep itself intact. But there are many additional points:

1. People who collaborate will be on the same page and understand the unique features of each person involved with a task. This makes it easier for those people to grow and evolve.

2. All the people who work together can do more things in less time. The burden of just one person having to complete lots of things at a time will be reduced.

3. Everyone can develop during a collaborative event. As people learn from each other, their individual skills will grow to allow the group to become more efficient over time.

Signs of a Collaborative Environment

There are many points to notice when looking at what makes a collaborative environment work with all the people involved feeling confident in what each other is doing at a moment.

1. Everyone in such an environment will start to feel happy about their work. They will notice there is a meaning in the things they are doing.

2. The work standards become stronger. Everyone notices that to succeed, they have to work together and get more done.

3. There is a balance between self-interest and team interest. People stop becoming selfish and think more about how an entire group will benefit. They know that when the group grows and thrives, the individuals will succeed just as well.

4. Everyone in the group is treated equally. Everyone in the situation will feel confident in what they are doing.

It is through these positives that people can start getting a business to grow and succeed. Several things can be done in this case to get people to move forward and feel better about what is going on.

Creating a Collaborative Environment

Building a workplace where people can collaborate and get along with one another is a vital part of emotional intelligence that anyone can use. There are several steps that can be used when producing an environment where everyone can feel supported:

1. Figure out the relationships between people in the workplace. See which people might get along with one another the best.

Look at the attributes of each person in the workplace to see how well they will get along with each other. Those who know how to work together will be stronger and more capable of moving forward in life.

2. Share plans with as many people in the workplace as possible.

The collaboration will not get anywhere when people are not fully aware of the plans being used. Everyone has to be aware of the things that are coming along in a situation. This includes looking at what people can do when working hard or making the most out of their efforts. People who are capable of working well in the workplace will be more likely to succeed.

3. Ask people about their feelings about working together.

Every employee will have their own beliefs or attitudes about working in a group. Some people might be excited about doing so. Others might be more reserved as they are not certain about what a task. People should be consulted so they can see what will happen in a working environment. The key is to look at how people feel about the situation and how changes can be made to fix things.

4. Look into the end results.

There is always a chance that the end result of a collaborative effort will be worthwhile. It could entail winning a game, getting more sales or just getting any major task completed. Every person will have an opinion on what a task means to them. Talk with each person about the end results to see what can happen and how issues might be resolved.

5. Establish a sense of mutual respect for everyone in the workplace.

Mutual respect is about letting people feel confident in what they have to do. When people feel respected, they will be ready to do anything. They know that they will not be criticized or slighted if they do things wrong. They will see that just making mistakes is part of the progressive learning experience.

Everything that works in a collaborative environment will be due to the emotional intelligence a leader exhibits. It is through that leader's work that people will know what they can do to get together and to become more productive.

Chapter 24 – Recognizing What a Team Can Do

Emotionally intelligent people are more likely to be leaders in a workplace. That is understandable because high EQ people have more control over their lives and know how to read the emotions of others while also managing their own.

A team must look at how well it is running and that a smart plan is used to get everyone on board to think carefully about how a task is to be done. There are several things a high EQ person can do when deciding what the members of a team can handle.

Review Motivations

Notice how workers in an environment engage one another. This includes understanding how people are motivated and how they might be encouraged to do things that they feel is for their benefit.

For example, Tony is working as a manager at a pizza delivery firm. He sees that Susan, a worker at the company, is putting in a great effort into what she is doing. She is handling the customer transactions well and can handle a computer with ease. She even has suggestions for how to keep tabs on some of the transactions made with regular customers. Tony might notice through Susan's work that she is highly motivated. She could work to do more things for the business like take care of the cash office. Tony understands that Susan's efforts are strong and that she is responsible.

Accountability Is Vital

A high EQ person will notice when others in a situation are accountable. That also involves knowing when others are doing the same.

Tony might see that Craig, another worker at the pizza place, is putting in an effort to manage pizza deliveries right. He is focusing on planning deliveries by reviewing the service coverage map and seeing which spots are the closest for him to deliver pizzas. He might even talk with others about seeing who should deliver pizzas to certain places. It is through this accountability that Craig is succeeding. By being accountable, he is showing that he understands the needs he has for taking care of more people in as little time as possible.

Linking With Others

Teamwork is a necessity in any working environment. A good way for someone to use emotional intelligence is to see how well people are communicating with each other and if they have good plans for interacting with each other.

Tony could try to get Susan and Craig to work together more often if he notices that they work well together. Susan might provide Craig with delivery and order information. Meanwhile, Craig will give her the money collected from each order while keeping it organized so she can process it.

By working with a collaborative approach, the two are showing that they get along with each other and understand their roles. The teamwork supported by the two will be vital to their success for going somewhere and getting more out of a job.

A high EQ person has to see how well people are working and that they can get along with each other well. Tony in this situation knows that there is a good connection between his employees, thus encouraging him to get those two to work together more often.

Looking into Empathy

People who show empathy will be more likely to stay strong and capable of expressing positive attitudes in the workplace.

A high EQ person must look at how individual workers express empathy. A person who focuses on good working relationships with others is someone who might be empathetic to others. Someone who helps others before oneself is also empathetic. Individuals can also be strong team players if they think about what they are doing to make their work focus on what they feel is right.

Potential Is the Key

No matter what one does when looking at everyone's role, it is vital for a high EQ person to look at a person's potential when getting more work done. Potential focuses not so much on what is happening right now but rather on what might happen later based on what people are doing in the workplace.

A high EQ person will think about how well a business can grow based on what someone sees in people. They will notice that people in an environment are working their hardest to get a business to grow and thrive. By working with high EQ people, a business can become easier to manage and operate.

Chapter 25 – How to Handle a Difficult Conversation

Conversations are a part of daily life that no one can ever truly ignore. Such events can take place in many forms. Sometimes they are face-to-face, but in other cases, they might be over the telephone or online. Conversations can be formal in nature or they might be casual between friends. There are many ways for people can communicate with each other, but in the end, a conversation is all about getting and receiving messages.

A good conversation can be easy to handle when all people are on the same page. It is in any discussion that people will understand what they can do to improve upon their lives and change things for the better. The problem though is that it is often a challenge to try to get through a conversation when it becomes intense. With the proper emotional intelligence, it becomes easier for people to feel confident and willing to move forward with their lives.

The greatest problem people have with many conversations is that they aren't aware of what they want to get out of them. They often forget about what makes their conversations valuable to each other.

There are several ways to manage a conversation. Knowing how to handle one's emotional intelligence can make a world of difference if planned right.

Notice the Subject

The first thing to do in a conversation is to think about the subject. The subject might not always be positive or comfortable for all people. The most important point is to avoid trying to change the subject.

A person with emotional intelligence will be ready to take on any challenge. This includes knowing how to work with difficult situations. Some people might try to change the subject or distract others from the main subject because they are not happy with it. A person can ask something like "How am I feeling about this subject?" By asking this, it becomes easier for a person to get in touch with one's feelings and attitudes.

Recognize the Emotions

By understanding the subject, it becomes easier to figure out the emotions that all people in a conversation are experiencing. At this point, the emotions must be recognized.

- Are people excited to talk about something?

- Is anyone afraid to talk about a subject?

- Who is trying to change the subject?

The key is to take the perspectives of those in the conversation. Ask them what they think about something and if they are comfortable with it. Notice the non-verbal cues that people are showing and this might help identify what someone is thinking or feeling.

In addition, emotions about a subject can change based on how familiar a person is with the content. The stress and worry that comes with a situation might be dramatic depending on what one is doing. By recognizing a person's emotions, it becomes easier for tasks to be discussed and for participants to decide what will make these experiences different or unique from one another.

Assess the Impact

Many emotions can trigger responses like the following:

- A desire to stay focused on a task

- Feelings of being overly analytical and judgmental

- Excessive criticism

- A need to look things in a certain fashion

Depending on what happens, the emotions might cause a person to want to engage in certain behaviors that are very different from what one might normally engage in.

Understand Where the Emotions Are Coming From

The emotions that people during a conversation can come from many sources. Some people might feel worried or nervous about certain things. They might be afraid of whatever it is they are entering into at the time. They might not fully recognize that what they want to do is sensible because they are fixated on certain outcomes that might be unrealistic.

A person with emotional intelligence will understand why people are feeling their emotions. These emotions might come from many sources:

- Preconceptions

- Stereotypes

- Previous events

- A desire to keep things the way they are

- General fear of something changing in some fashion

A person will have to talk with others about their feelings and what is causing them. This produces empathy as a person recognizes what is causing someone to act in a certain way. Having empathy, in this case, is vital for producing a positive atmosphere or climate where everyone involved feels positive.

Resolve Certain Problems

There must be a plan to resolve issues that occur. Understanding the issues that others have is a good start. There needs to be a plan to figure out what can be done next.

There are a few steps that may be used:

1. Look into the problem someone has.

2. Ask that person about the problem. What is causing that issue?

3. Discover the person's competencies. Maybe they have issues that are keeping him or her from completing a task.

4. Find a solution for that problem. This includes understanding what can be done to help people feel comfortable with what they are doing.

5. See if the person can handle the solution. The effort must be based on one's skills and ability to make it work.

Working with a difficult conversation can be a real challenge. When the right plans are utilized and one's emotional intelligence is utilized, it becomes easier for problems to be resolved the right way. Having a good plan to keep problems in check can make a world of difference.

Chapter 26 – The Pain of Lies (and How to Identify Them)

It is uncertain as to when the first lie was told, but it is clear that lying is something that people do all the time. People lie to get their way or to keep things in a certain situation from being worse. Lies are not things that people are comfortable with, and yet they are constantly done by people who want to get out of the problems they find themselves in. It is only second nature for people to lie about things.

Lying is not something that people like to deal with. It is up to someone with emotional intelligence to identify when a person is lying. The key is to not only figure out who isn't telling the truth but to also help that person who might be going through something difficult and this has led to a lie being told.

Why Do People Lie? (and What These Reasons Mean)

People tell lies for many reasons.

1. Some people lie to try and deflect responsibilities.

For instance, Jim might be told to complete a certain task at the supermarket where he works. He might be told to clean out the fridge, but he is not comfortable with walking into the chilled space to do it. Therefore, he might lie to another worker and say that he or she has to take care of the job. This is an example of how a person might want to skirt tasks.

Lying, in this case, is an indication that someone is not responsible. Jim might not be responsible enough to do certain tasks. Therefore, he is cheating his way out of being responsible. He needs to be consulted regarding the importance of being responsible.

2. They are afraid of what might happen if they tell the truth.

Let's go back to the supermarket to look at Susan, a customer service employee who ran into an issue with a customer. She was not doing well with a customer who was frustrated. At the same time, Susan was getting increasingly frustrated too. In this case, the customer got upset and wrote an angry message on the customer service survey on her receipt. That customer wrote Susan's name and complained about her. The manager talked to Susan about this situation. Susan lied and said that the customer was being irate and she was trying to be reasonable with her. In reality, she contributed to the problem. Susan did this out of fear. She was worried about what could happen. Perhaps she might be more interested in having a consistent life on the job where she knows what is going to happen. She had a concern that by being talked to by the manager, her relationship with the manager would change.

3. They are uncertain what to do with their lives.

It is easy for anyone to become worried and fearful of what they want to do. When a person lies, that person is trying to keep the status quo. This includes trying to keep a subject from being explored.

There are also times when a person might lie to avoid having to respond to something. People who are afraid of what they might have to encounter or discuss will lie based on one's personal needs.

4. A person wants to have more control.

Many people who lie do so because they want to maintain control. Jim and Susan at the market might have gotten into an argument over what they want to do in the workplace. They have their own ideas for what they feel is right and appropriate for the business.

One of the two might lie during the dispute. Either Jim or Susan could lie because one of them feels that the truth is not going to support one's views. When the truth clashes with a desire, it becomes easier for someone's narrative to be shut down. As this happens, that person ends up losing control over the discussion because of a desire to control the debate.

5. People lie because they don't want to disappoint others.

When Susan was talking with a manager about some issue that took place she lied about what happened when she was talking with a customer. While she might have been worried about her relationship with someone changing, there is an even bigger point that may be explored. In this case, Susan might have been afraid of disappointing the manager. The manager might have been unhappy with the situation, but at least that person would be fine with Susan if she was just open and truthful about what happened.

When Susan tries to lie, it makes the situation worse. She is aware of what other people think about her. She doesn't want people to judge her for what she is doing or how she is living her life.

6. People often distort their realities to believe that the lies they tell are true.

Living in a mindset where the truth doesn't exist sounds convenient. A person might want to avoid the truth. By not acknowledging the truth, that person is changing their reality. People do this out of a desire to feel more positive. They want narratives to go alongside their own attitudes and opinions. In short, people might lie because they aren't responsible or maybe they have fears about what can happen when something uncertain comes along. Their images are important for them to protect because they do not want to be seen in a negative light.

7. Lying is often done out of convenience.

It is often difficult for people to make explanations over whatever it is they are doing. Therefore, they often try to shift the blame to others. They make up stories to make it easier for them to keep people from asking questions.

These lies are difficult, but they are concerns that must be explored in detail regardless of what is and is not real. Knowing about lies is vital for building one's emotional intelligence. A person with a high EQ will understand what a person is doing when lying. It becomes easier for someone to identify when a person is worried.

Gaining Trust

It only takes a few moments for a person to lie about things. All those lies can add up to the point that someone is not easy to trust. It is not hard to gain a person's trust when plans are made to get the cycle of lying to finally stop.

An important point about using one's EQ to identify lies is to help break the cycle of lying and to create a sense of trust among people. While a simple lie might sound like a good idea for someone at the start, that lie can become problematic.

When a person tells a lie, that person will feel happy knowing that he or she is getting one's way. After that lie happens, that person would have to tell another lie later. The second lie would support the first one. A third lie to bolster the other two would be told, and so forth. Eventually, it becomes difficult to try and keep the lie running, thus leading to the whole thing falling apart.

The biggest problem is that a person who consistently lies will eventually be hard to trust. When those lies are exposed, that person will not be someone people want to trust. If anything, a person who admits to just one lie might be seen as a habitual liar who will keep on lying no matter what happens. This problem establishes a sense of distrust where a person will be impossible to trust later on.

A person who uses one's EQ to identify lies can work to understand what is causing a person to tell those lies. This includes working to find ways for a person to get away from those lies. By working with this, that person's reputation can start to be built back up again.

How to Tell When a Person Is Lying

Lies are easy for people to tell all the time. It is often easier for people to tell lies and to get away with them when they know what they are doing. People who lie and can get away with it are among the strongest people as they can manipulate others. By managing one's emotional intelligence, it becomes easier for someone to figure out when a person is lying. This makes it easier for someone to confront another person about the lies that are being told and what can be done to keep those lies from being any worse than they already are.

Using one's ability to handle nonverbal communication is vital to identifying when a person is lying. Nonverbal communication is a good part of EQ that helps to find even the smallest cues suggesting that a person is lying.

There are some commonplace signs that a person is nervous and worried about what one is doing when they are lying.

1. A person is changing their head position quickly.

When a person lies, he or she might express some cues like looking nervous or hesitant. That person will try to keep one's face from being visible and will want to change one's head position often. The head might move in many directions:

- The head will go in the opposite direction.

- It may also be retracted as someone tries to keep the head closer to the rest of the body.

- A person could also bend the head back to keep one's visual cues from being easy to spot.

2. Certain parts of the body are being covered up.

When a person covers the body, that someone does this to try and keep signs of lying from being visible. This could include a person hiding one's feelings of being worried or nervous. It may also be to hide feelings of relief when a lie is accepted and no one questions it.

The cover-up is often as easy to notice as the lie.

- A liar might try to cover one's mouth or throat.

- A liar might keep the chest covered to try and keep their heavy breathing from being noticed.

- The exposed skin around the arms might be covered. A person could keep one's arms folded to keep someone from seeing the hairs on the arms sticking up.

3. The body appears to look agitated or completely still while lying.

One of the more telltale signs of someone lying is the body is shaking. This comes from a person trying to hide one's efforts to lie. The opposite is also true. A liar might try to keep one's body still while in the act.

The best way to compare the two is through the fight-or-flight attitude. When someone stands still when lying, that person is showing a will to fight and to use a lie to get one's way. When that person is agitated and shaking, that person has a flight approach where he or she is lying to get out of something that person does not want to enter into.

These are signs that one's body is being positioned in a way to keep one's true intentions from being visible. A good example of this can be seen when a person is shuffling their feet. As the feet start moving, it becomes clear that a person is trying to hide something. The liar becomes nervous and worried about what will happen next and will start to shake one's feet and move around a bit. That person wants to get out of the conversation and will try anything to skirt away from it.

4. Changes in breathing.

A person who lies will start to breathe heavily because they will feel a stress reflex when lying. The person who does this will try to make the lie sound credible. The effort to make that lie sound authentic will cause that person to try and hold their breath or to stay looking as normal as possible. The gradual changes in one's breathing are signs of a person being fearful of what is happening in a situation. Knowing how to manage those fears and to see what is happening can make a difference when finding ways to help people.

The changes in one's breathing will result in many things:

- The voice might start to sound shallow.

- The shoulders will begin to rise.

- The breathing sounds are much easier to identify. Heavy breathing can be heard from a few feet away.

- A person's mouth might hang open for a brief moment.

These stresses occur because a person has a higher heart rate and is uncertain about what will happen. It can be a struggle to keep the lie sounding credible.

5. Certain words or phrases might be repeated consistently.

A liar will have a specific script for espousing the fiction. The script includes a series of phrases or specific words used to try to keep the lie intact and consistent. A person might use the same words in a lie to try and buy some time. They trying to gather their thoughts and keep the lie sounding as authentic as possible.

For instance, a worker might try to get out of his job early and would concoct a lie. He might have a plan to say "I have to get to the airport to pick up someone," but when he does this, he might say "I have...I have to get to the airport. I need to go to the airport to pick up someone. Can I go early to the airport?"

In this example, he is trying to reinforce that he supposedly needs to get to the airport. A person with a low EQ might assume that he is desperate and serious about this and that he needs to reach someone as quickly as possible. Someone with a high EQ will know that he is just trying to gather his emotions. He is looking to keep himself from looking nervous, and as a result, is adding more words unnecessarily. In this case, he is using the same words as a means of bolstering the lie.

6. The information being provided is too extensive.

People talk often when they are lying because they desperately want to get people to believe what they are saying. A person who genuinely needs to leave work early might say something like "I need to leave early so I can pick someone up at the airport." The boss might understand this, especially if that person can identify that the person saying this isn't expressing other signs of lying.

The man who wanted to con his way out of work early might say something a little too detailed. He might say, "I need to get out of work so I can pick up my brother from the airport. He's coming in from Denver and I got to catch him. He's coming in an hour."

215

All that detail is not necessary especially if the request is just simple and that person doesn't need to explain too much. For the liar, in this case, he will desperately try to tell people that he needs to get out and include some very specific things in his lie. He sounds like he has a good plan in mind, but in reality, he is desperately trying to build up his lie to make it sound all the more appealing.

7. It just becomes very hard for a person to speak while lying.

All the pressure of a person trying to lie and be convincing might cause that person to emotionally break down and they are too nervous or frustrated to speak.

The man who is trying to cut out of work might be struggling with his words. In addition to repeating some of those words, he might struggle with saying them. He might start to use more syllables for certain words, for instance, "ai-r-port."

Identifying a liar is not only about having a strong EQ but also identifying a person's physical response. The liar might have less saliva. When a person is in a high-stress situation, the nervous system produces less saliva. The mouth becomes dry, thus making it hard for some words to be spoken.

How to Use One's EQ to Identify and Confront a Liar

It is through one's emotional intelligence that it is easy for a liar to be detected. A person who has a strong EQ will have an easier time with not only finding a liar but also talking with that person. The most important thing to do when confronting a liar is not to publicly shame that person or to get upset. A person with a strong EQ will want to get to the bottom of the situation. This includes looking at what is causing a person to lie.

The goal is to get that person to not only stop lying but to also change their attitudes and values about lying.

1. Look at what one is saying or doing. Remember if a person hesitates when speaking or volunteers too much information can be a sign of lying.

2. Try to analyze that person's body movements. They could be still or agitated in appearance.

3. Try to confirm before starting a confrontation that the suspected lie is indeed a lie. Always check one's sources and see if there are any inconsistencies.

4. When talking to a liar, do not be hostile or confrontational. A person who is angry or upset might make the situation worse.

5. The facts should be gathered to confirm that a person is indeed lying.

6. Ask questions about the lie. Be as specific as possible. Asking questions helps uncover the reasons for why a person is lying. The person may not be able to keep his statements straight.

7. Show empathy when addressing the lie. This includes knowing how a person is feeling and why that person might have lied.

8. Discuss what can be done to control the lying in the future.

It is important for a liar to stop, but it takes a bit of time for that person to become trustworthy again. There has to be a plan for that person to avoid lying in the future. A simple discussion can be held to figure out what should work to keep that person from lying and getting into even more trouble.

Be willing to reflect upon the situation. The reflection period allows the liar to understand the harm that they have caused others due to the lie. This causes that person to see that the lie being told was wrong and that it should have been avoided. Knowing this, the person will see that lying is no longer worth it. They will start to be honest in the future, thus rebuilding the trust that someone might hold.

Chapter 27 – The Betari Box

A good way to build one's emotional intelligence is to use the Betari Box. It is a box that relates to how a person's behaviors and attitudes influence the actions of those in a local area.

The Betari Box focuses on who is doing what they can to make a positive impact on their lives and the lives of other people around them. By working with the Betari Box, a person aiming to develop their EQ will quickly notice that there are reasons why people act in certain ways.

The Betari Cycle

The Betari Box is a basic cycle that has four parts that go into a box shape:

1. Mr. X's attitude will affect his behavior.

2. Mr. X's behavior will affect Mrs. Y's attitude.

3. Mrs. Y's attitude affects her behavior.

4. Mrs. Y's behavior affects Mr. X's attitude.

When someone has a difficult attitude, it will influence their behavior and that of everyone else.

Here is an example of how the Betari Box works. Sarah and Troy are working at an airport. They are both trying to get passengers to move through a security gate as quickly as possible. The two want people to get to their flights and to avoid having to wait in security for too long. To make it all work, they need to be positive.

Sarah might have a positive attitude. She feels happy about her work and that she is making a difference by being friendly to the people who come into the airport. Therefore, she will exhibit positive behaviors. Sarah will be cordial to the people who come in without sounding impersonal. She would be nice to the kids that come along and even acknowledge the pets that might be carried aboard a plane.

Those positive behaviors that Sarah engages in will cause Troy to feel happy. He will see that she is positive, and in turn, will start to feel happy himself. He will know that there's a good atmosphere in the workplace, thus leading him into performing positive things and actions for people at the security gate. He will talk with the people, kindly instruct them about security practices, and so forth.

All that positivity from Troy will rub off on Sarah as she continues to be happy. The cycle of the Betari Box keeps moving, thus allowing them to get along and to have a great experience at the airport.

What if Sarah wasn't happy and was being rude to the people who come through security? She might become judgmental. Troy would start to act the same way as he begins to see that the work environment isn't as peaceful or positive as he might have wished it could be.

How Are the Emotions of the Betari Box Conveyed?

The Betari Box can be noticed in action based on many things, such as:

- All the people in the workplace might be active or sluggish.

- The communications people have can make an impact. Sometimes the people are all getting along, but in other cases, they might be removed from each other or impersonal in how they are talking to each other.

- People might express the same tones in their voices or in their facial expressions.

- The attitudes and emotions of people can have ups and downs. People might start to feel happy at the beginning of the day, but after a while, everyone will feel tired. The Betari Box is in action when everyone's moods and behaviors are changing at once.

The Betari Box shows that people are often united in how they are acting. Those who have a strong EQ will notice that there is always going to be some case where introducing one action to a few people will cause them to change the ways they work, thus changing what everyone else in the workplace is doing.

The Main Principle

The Betari Box shows not only how an atmosphere can change but also in how people might perceive things in certain ways. When one person notices a certain behavior or action, it becomes easy for changes to be made.

Going back to the start, Sarah might act positively toward Troy and other people in an area. Troy will interpret this as a sign of friendship. He is influenced by Sarah because he noticed that her behaviors are what people should be doing in the workplace. Therefore, Troy will act positively toward Sarah and everyone else who comes by. The cycle of feelings is produced as the two people start to get in touch with each other and feel confident about being in one another's presence.

The cycle generated within the Betari Box is where decisions are made and actions take place. Knowing how the box is formed and how people can respond to each other through it is a necessity for recognizing what one might be doing in a situation.

How to Manage the Betari Box

Knowing how to work with the Betari Box and to use it to one's advantage is a necessity for having a good relationship with anyone. There are several things that can be done to get the Betari Box managed properly:

1. Be aware of the attitudes that are produced.

A person in a workplace will have to notice their attitude and the attitudes of people around them. These include positive and negative attitudes. Knowing what the attitudes are like makes it easier for people to plan efforts based on what they feel is suitable for better behaviors.

2. Identify how those attitudes affect someone's behavior.

Sometimes the attitudes might cause real changes over what someone is doing in the workplace. When one man is happy and joyful, he starts to feel more energetic. He feels great about himself and wants to let other people feel just as happy as he is.

3. Analyze the behaviors of others. Figure out what is causing them to express such feelings.

Everyone has their own feelings that make them say or do certain things. Knowing how to review those feelings and actions is vital to recognize what can be done in a work environment.

4. Try to talk with those people about why their emotions are the way they are.

Having a good EQ enables a person to ask people about their emotions and why they are feeling certain ways.

5. Find ways for someone to be more positive.

It helps to talk to someone about how the positive attitudes one has can make life better and easier for everyone involved.

Having an idea of how to manage the Betari Box and to keep people from expressing the wrong emotions is a necessity for moving forward.

Chapter 28 – Building Accountability

Having a clear and focused mind is critical to success in the workplace or in any relationship one is trying to have. Accountability is a part of emotional intelligence that makes a difference. A person with a high EQ is willing to be accountable. This includes not only the actions one engages in but also the emotions and feelings that others start to feel.

Accountability is a part of EQ that causes a person to develop strong relationships with others and be appreciated and supported by others. When someone is accountable, that person is honest and willing to take the lead. In many cases, that person is more rational because he or she knows that what is being done is that person's responsibility.

People appreciate others who are accountable. Those people who are responsible for what they are doing will be admired for being honest and direct with others.

Taking Ownership

The basic point about accountability is that a person is showing a sense of responsibility. An accountable person is ready to take ownership of whatever they are doing. The key is to show that someone understands what is happening and what might be changing in any environment.

When something good happens because of someone's actions, that person is willing to acknowledge their role. This includes showing a sense of interest or concern for other people in an environment.

When something negative happens because of what someone is doing, that person will not try to shift the blame or make excuses. Instead, they will take responsibility and find a way to correct any issues.

Those who take ownership are emotionally strong because they know that what they are doing will impact the feelings of others. The key is to do things that will make people feel better while correcting anything that goes in the opposite direction.

People who are not willing to take ownership of their thoughts or actions will be seen in a different light. Those people will feel unhappy and not willing to work together.

How to Develop Accountability

The process of building accountability is critical for building EQ. Several things can be done to become a more accountable person.

1. Show a sense of humility.

People who are humble already know what they are really like. A person will not blame other people when things don't go as planned. A person will be honest and ready to acknowledge their faults.

2. Decide on one's responsibility.

Emotions can develop when responsibilities are known. They know what they need to care about the most and are ready to avoid dwelling too long on the things that do not matter.

3. Life has to be managed.

People need to look at how they can schedule their lives. A well-managed life allows a person to be productive. Not everyone can handle lots of tasks at the same time. By handling one's life with care and control, it becomes easier for someone to avoid problems. A schedule can be planned ahead of time. Having a schedule ready allows a person to know what may be done and when.

4. Avoid committing to too many things.

It is easy for people to take in more work than what they can handle. Sometimes a person who commits to a work project might not be able to do it all.

For instance, a man at an office might be told to work on a payroll report. He might also ask to work on some contracts for new hires as well as communications with outside vendors. This man is accepting too many jobs at once. While he feels that he is capable of doing more, he is not ready to do all those jobs at the same time. As a result, they will break down and become harder to trust because that person cannot be seen as accountable.

Having the power to say "no" or to just manage one's time the right way is a critical skill that must be learned and practiced.

Chapter 29 – Remaining Calm Under Pressure

It only takes a few moments for a good situation to go haywire. As pressure builds up, it is harder for people to work. This is not the case for high EQ people. One part of emotional intelligence is knowing how to remain calm even in a high-pressure situation. People who have a high EQ are capable of managing high-pressure events.

It is understandable as to why people might break under intense pressure. People might be uncertain about what might happen. For instance, a person might be told to complete a task in 24 hours even though it might realistically take 36 hours to do it. That added time crunch can cause a person to feel pressure.

A person with a low EQ would simply avoid trying to get work done at this point. That person would probably be more interested in something like just resting or relaxing one's mind without doing anything.

Those who have high EQ levels will feel more confident with what they are doing. They will not feel as much stress while in high-pressure events. They will know that they can handle anything that might be difficult and that they will make it through even the most complicated situation that might be given to them.

Be Positive

The first thing that can be done to remain calm is to stay positive. A high EQ person will notice that there is always a good thing to come out of an assignment no matter how rough it gets.

People who are not emotionally developed are more likely to jump to conclusions and assume that everything happening is not worthwhile and that they are only going to get into even more trouble as they try to change things.

People with better EQ ratings are different. An emotionally smart person will know that every situation has multiple sides. They continue to work toward having a better and more enjoyable life, and part of this involves seeing the bright side.

Staying positive not only makes it easier for a person to think but also improves how well a person might react to something unexpected. More importantly, the brain will start to move into a more positive mindset where it is harder for stress-related chemicals like cortisol to be produced. Having a relaxed and clear mind is vital to keeping one's life from being any harder than it needs to be.

Avoid Playing the Victim

It is through accountability that people are capable of making the right decisions and choices. To make one's life easier, it is important for a person to avoid thinking they are the victim of a situation. Anyone can play the victim. Those people who do that aren't going to contribute anything valuable. A professional victim will let a sense of disappointment cloud their judgment.

The important thing is that it is possible for a person to respond to the issues in a positive way. The best way to build EQ is to think about everything that is contributing to a problem and to find a way to resolve the issue before it gets worse. This will go a long way toward being stronger and in control.

Establish a Perspective

It is through a strong perspective that a person is capable of staying confident and is able to understand what is happening in a situation. Having a good perspective helps a person to keep one's mind intact without worrying about the stresses that come with trying to complete certain tasks.

A good way to build one's EQ is to look at the things that are causing a situation to happen. The odds are there is a very good reason why a situation is happening. It could be from outside factors that one is not fully aware of. By growing one's EQ, it becomes easier for a person to have an easier time controlling stressful or pressure-filled situations.

Those who are emotionally weak do not think about the perspectives of others. They assume that everything is all about them, thus hurting their chances to get things done. However, by working with a sense of perspective, it becomes easier for someone to start looking at other things.

Chapter 30 – Managing Anger

Anyone who says that he or she is never angry is likely not telling the truth. The fact is that anger can be a problem that will develop in anyone's mind.

When a person is in a traffic jam, they may become angry. They desperately want to get to their destination on time, but it becomes hard to deal with the stress and hassle that comes with the traffic jam. Therefore, that someone will become very angry over the situation.

Maybe someone gets passed over for a promotion or raise. Perhaps a machine in the office is not working like it is supposed to. Whatever the problem might be, there are always reasons as to why someone can become angry.

Anger is not always easy to predict. Anger can come about at any time. It only takes a few moments for a person to go from being grounded and in control to be overly upset with whatever is happening.

It is through one's emotional intelligence that it might become easier for a person's anger to be kept in check without becoming a huge threat. There are many things that have to be done to keep anger under control.

Ways to Correct Issues Surrounding Anger

There are several things that can be done to control one's anger, but these strategies have to be used carefully so there are no problems with managing one's emotions or thoughts.

1. Get one's composure back.

Anger can dominate the brain like no other emotion can. When a person is angry, it becomes easy for them to become really frustrated and upset. Anger makes it harder for someone to think rationally because the anger takes over.

The best thing to do when gaining emotional intelligence is to find a way to get over the anger. This can include figuring out strategies for managing one's anger and knowing how to get beyond it. The amount of time it takes for a person's anger to cool and become relaxed again can vary according to how disciplined they are.

2. Avoid deflecting the issues onto other people.

It is easy for people to try to deflect the problems they have onto others. People often do this to make it easier for them to get away with things. Deflecting problems and making other people handle them is only going to make the situation worse.

A high EQ person must avoid making their problems another's burden. Keeping a perspective and attempt to understand the problems and what caused the problems to arise.

3. Think about what one wants to say first.

Anyone who is angry will have a clouded mindset. That person will stop thinking rational thoughts and focus more on trying to take one's anger out on other people. Doing so makes the situation worse.

Instead, a high EQ person can think about something that can be said to defuse the situation. Part of this strategy involves thinking about the consequences of being angry.

Plan a smart response that shows respect and offers a solution. Don't blame anyone for the situation.

4. Explain things carefully and directly.

There is always a reason why a person might be angry. Sometimes it might be more rational than one could expect. When the problem in mind does become easy to understand and express, a person can express things clearly. A person must talk directly to others about what is causing the frustration. Be calm and rational.

5. Find solutions to the anger.

Anger is only a temporary feeling so long as the angry person thinks about what can be done to fix the problem. Solutions for lessening the anger can be found when talking out the situation. Any kind of solution can be suggested. Looking into how such problems might be solved is a sign of maturity.

6. Be willing to see the lighter side.

People who think too hard about their situations might be frustrated and difficult to work with. There is always a bright side to whatever is happening. A high EQ person will concentrate on the positive or lighter things of something that is happening. Maybe a difficult task is something that will build one's skills. Perhaps there is something amusing about a situation that makes it more interesting and less threatening.

7. Follow through with one's plan to resolve the anger.

Sometimes the efforts needed to get over the anger will only take a few moments to complete. Having everything down pat to fix the issues at hand will be worthwhile for all people to work with. Learning how to control one's anger can help anyone get beyond the most difficult problems. Besides, a person who is angry will not get much done in life.

Passive-Aggressive Anger

Passive-aggressive anger is a form of anger that may be worse than overt anger. It is through passive-aggressive anger that a person might become difficult to manage or hard to communicate with. It may also be harder to detect.

Passive-aggressive anger occurs when a person is upset or angry, but they express it indirectly. For instance, a person might make a comment that someone is not happy about. That comment might be interpreted as a direct jab at someone in particular. Instead of showing anger, the passive-aggressive person will find a way of being difficult in a quiet way. They may be angry but it will not be shown as an overt action.

Managing passive-aggressive anger is to not only think about the source of the anger but the reason why someone erupted in anger. People have to look at what they are thinking and what they can do to change their mindsets before their feelings of anger become worse.

In most cases, the person who caused the anger to develop has no ill will toward a person. Being angry is going to impose the wrong message on someone and make that person feel guilty and angry over time.

High EQ people are more adept at keeping anger from being a threat, especially when it comes to passive-aggressive anger.

Chapter 31 – Using Emotional Intelligence When Planning a Team

It is through teamwork that people can get things done. Every team is different based on its skills and attributes, but any team can succeed regardless of how it is built. Emotional intelligence may be used to create a strong team that is suitable for any task.

This chapter looks into the many ways how people can use their emotional intelligence to handle what is happening in a workplace. Having a good plan for managing emotional intelligence can help people to grow and become stronger together.

Every team has to include only the right people who understand what they are required to do. Multiple steps can be used with one's EQ to see how well a team can be organized.

1. Every team must have a leader.

Although all members of a team are important, a certain person should be chosen as a leader to get the team to work well and support everyone. A leader can be chosen according to their ability to resolve conflicts and desire to listen.

A high EQ person can review individuals and assign them to leadership positions based on how well they listen and support others while also respecting the attributes of individual team members. The leader must be able to control and direct the actions of the team and keep the team motivated and cohesive.

2. Review the strengths of each team member.

A high EQ person will take note of the strengths of all other people in a group after a leader is chosen. Every skill should be reviewed based on these factors:

- How well a person does certain tasks

- How long it takes for those tasks to be completed

- An individual's interest in completing certain jobs

- How consistent a person is with managing jobs

- Flexibility based on someone's capability of going from one task to another

- The ability of a person to handle pressure and time constraints

3. Create a series of norms for people to have.

The norms in the group should be agreed upon by everyone involved. These norms are a series of rules relating to what people will do to accomplish the task at hand.

The norms can include a series of ground rules like what people in certain positions must do, how others will report to one another and when they need to finish certain tasks. The leader will understand who is capable of handling tasks and who might have to be moved from one part of a group to another.

4. Give everyone a voice.

Every member of the group should be allowed a voice in what can be done and how to accomplish the tasks given to the group.

5. Determine if people are willing to work together.

A group works best when all people involved are willing to work together. A team must be planned so that the members are comfortable with each other and there are no antagonistic people to cause disruption. Those who are able to manage their emotions well will be more likely to go accomplish more.

6. Understand the ways members communicate with one another.

Everyone in the group should know how to communicate with one another and be willing to do so. It is through communication that people are capable of accomplishing more together.

Chapter 32 – Using Emotional Intelligence Ethically

People are always trying to find ways to make their lives better. People need to be aware of what they are doing when helping others. There needs to be a sense of ethics involved with how people handle certain things in their lives. Being aware of the emotional considerations that come with one's life includes working with ethics in mind.

Emotional intelligence is something that people can use for the greater good. By using one's EQ, a person can help others and manage some of the stressful or difficult things that can come along. People use their EQ skills to address issues that people have and to make them feel better. In some cases, EQ works with self-help intentions. Those who use EQ to their advantage will feel better about themselves because they know they are doing things right for others and giving people the support they need.

Emotional intelligence can be abused by people. Practically anything relating to communication and interacting with others can be abused in some fashion. Still, it is harsh when something that should be as positive as EQ is utilized in a way that might hurt others.

Sometimes a person can use their emotional intelligence to manipulate a situation and to make things go a certain way. An example of this could be seen in an accounting office. George is struggling to handle a few tax documents for some small businesses. Roger insists that George use a few shortcuts and omit some details and maybe add some filler numbers into a report. Although this might allow the task to be completed sooner, it is unethical because it is not the truth about what businesses are doing.

Roger might use his emotional intelligence to convince George that it is perfectly fine for him to skirt his way around some reports. Roger might see that George is tired and frustrated and wants to find a way to eliminate some of the problems he has. Roger might even coax him into thinking about how he would feel when all those struggles he has might disappear.

In a perfect world, Roger would use his emotional intelligence to encourage George to keep on working and to think about finishing his task. Instead, George has been goaded into breaking the rules because doing so might be convenient.

This is an example of how emotional intelligence can be abused. This is a problem that many people fall into when using their emotional intelligence because while they think what they are doing is right, it is not necessarily something that will be to the benefit of others.

It is a necessity for people to be aware of what they are doing when using their emotional intelligence to their advantage. The main goal of using emotional intelligence is to keep from abusing it. Several points should be explored relating to how this works in life.

The Dumbstruck Effect

The dumbstruck effect is a process where a person who gives an emotion-filled speech will have their message heard. This can be either good or bad. For instance, Martin Luther King Jr.'s many speeches and sermons were filled with intense emotion. He was known for being attuned to the words he was saying and wanted people to pay attention to everything. The work that he put into his speeches helped people take his words seriously. More importantly, they were vital for advancing much of the civil rights narrative of his time.

On the other end of things, some of the speeches that Adolf Hitler gave as he took control of Germany were about being divisive and militant. He convinced others to believe one group of people was ethically and morally superior to others. People who followed Hitler were willing to do so even if the things he believed were unsustainable and dangerous. The emotion he conveyed helped make him more convincing and made people eager to follow him and believe everything he was saying.

In the cases of both King and Hitler, people were dumbstruck. There was a heightened sense of emotion that they put into what they were saying. That added emotion prompted people to think in certain ways and to want to follow.

Through the dumbstruck effect, people can get their way if they know how to play with emotions. While it can be used for good to encourage people to do positive things like in King's case, it can also be dangerous like with what Hitler was discussing.

Anyone with a high EQ must think about the impact that one has on other people who listen. Understanding these impacts is vital.

A Focus on Personal Gain (Machiavellianism)

Machiavellianism is a practice where a person focuses on personal gain and their own interest in all things.

This is being self-centered. A person who follows this concept is going to think less about other people and more about what one can get. Those who can manage their actions through Machiavellianism will be doing so with their own values and beliefs in mind.

The concept is named for Niccolo Machiavelli, an Italian writer who had been exiled from political functions not long before he wrote the Prince in 1513. His book was notorious for including discussions on dishonest and harmful behavior toward others and how people would often use those actions to get their way and to take power. The book is believed to be a guide for how to cheat their way to success and to move forward in spite of others. Whether or not Machiavelli intended for his book to do that is unclear, but the tactics he discussed are often used by people who have a strong sense of emotional intelligence.

People who use their EQ for personal gain or engage in Machiavellianism often hold many emotions and values:

1. People are often motivated based on what they feel is the most beneficial to them.

A person might engage in actions simply out of what they feel is necessary for them. It does not matter if other people are harmed or at risk or in danger. A Machiavellian person will think more about earning money, having power over people, and simply winning above all else by any means necessary.

Those who exhibit this are not likely to feel concerned with building communities or friendships. They might not even think about the emotions of other people. To them, it is through their own emotions that they are guided.

2. People can predict what others might think.

It is very easy for a person with Machiavellian tendencies to predict what someone else might be thinking. They might be able to predict what people would say when they are engaging in certain actions and habits. When someone can predict what is happening with someone else, it becomes easy for that person to manipulate the outcomes of certain situations.

3. It is through one's self-image that many decisions are made.

A person's self-image is what inspires certain actions to take place. A person might make choices based on what someone thinks is appropriate for one's image.

A Machiavellian will use one's EQ to find ways to make them look better to others. A person feels others will respect them for what they can offer. It can be a form of bribery.

4. Sometimes other people can be treated as obstacles or tools as a means to an end.

A Machiavellian person will use other people to achieve a goal. This includes taking advantage of the resources, the things they say and any other actions. The hostile person takes advantage of others who are unsuspecting. A Machiavellian person can directly influence what someone might do or engage in harmful behaviors to change the lives of others.

Distorting the Truth

People with a high EQ have the ability to manipulate the truth. This is a little different from outright lying in that a person might be telling a truth but could be doing so with a few alterations or fabrications. A person who distorts the truth will spread rumors or other falsehoods within the truth. These are often produced to try and create an advantage. The unconfirmed information might be conveyed in a manner that makes it sounds true. As a result, it might be easy for a person who listens to be convinced that the falsehoods being said are truths.

Sometimes a person will lie to protect someone or to give another person some kind of benefit. In most cases, people will lie with their personal benefits in mind.

Ethical Standards

By working with the right ethical standards, it becomes easier for a person to know how to avoid problems and to get along with other people in an appropriate and sensible fashion.

1. It is important to focus on the positive and productive things that someone can do.

People who use their emotional intelligence must do so with positive intentions. This includes helping people to see the benefits of certain things or to be constructive in the workplace or any other area.

2. Be realistic when talking about things from an emotional standpoint.

3. A person who uses one's emotional intelligence should be an advocate for others.

Emotional intelligence is ideal for when someone is trying to stand up for someone. This includes speaking out for people who might not have the ability to do so themselves.

4. Never try to tear people down when speaking to them.

Bullying and other actions where people are insulted or mocked are never beneficial. Some people use their emotional intelligence to subject people to mockery and insults. Most often the people who are being mocked or hassled in the name of emotional intelligence do not deserve it. Never talk down to people or insult them. Other people have feelings and the things that make them very different are issues that they do not have any real control over.

5. Understand how other people feel when emotional intelligence is used.

It is easy for people who have high EQ levels to forget about the people that they are impacting. Although anyone can benefit from a high EQ, some people might hurt others without intending to. Help others to understand what they can do to stay confident and comfortable. The potential for someone to develop feelings of remorse are often strong and should not be discounted when trying to complete a task with a larger group.

Working with ethics in one's emotional intelligence is a necessity. It is through ethical behaviors that it becomes easier for people to manage their emotions and to be in full control of whatever it is they are saying or doing.

Is It Ever Fine to Mislead People?

Some people might argue that it is perfectly fine to use one's EQ to mislead others. They may think that doing so is for the better good of another person. That does not mean it is always the right thing to do.

For instance, Tom might tell Roger that he needs to consider selling his house and getting a smaller one. Tom could lie to Roger by convincing him that the value of his home is going to decline and that he should find a smaller and cheaper property before it is too late. In reality, the market might be stable. Roger might think that it is fine to sell his home. In reality, Tom might do this to buy the home at a certain value before its property goes up. In other words, Tom is misleading Roger for his own benefit and not Roger's.

This is not an ethical use of emotional intelligence. Tom is taking advantage of Roger's gullibility. He knows that Roger can be quickly misled if the right words or actions are used. Tom, if he is honest, might encourage Roger to look the market to see if this is a good time to sell. Tom would be suggesting selling the house but would not go as far as to recommend that he do it.

Someone might mislead another person into doing something that requires someone to go to the hospital for a doctor's visit. Maybe they might scare someone into thinking he or she has some medical condition. This might be done to coax a person into going to the doctor for a routine visit. Instead of misleading the person, it is better to explain directly what they should do. This is a more ethical way of using one's EQ as it focuses on a direct communication with someone without adding pressure or telling an untruth. The parties involved will be open with each other and therefore more likely to trust each other.

In short, it is a terrible idea to mislead someone using your EQ even if it is for positive intentions. Being direct and honest while expressing one's EQ is the best thing that can be done.

Chapter 33 – Questions to Ask About Emotional Intelligence

Those who work hard on improving their emotional intelligence will feel more confident about themselves and capable of helping others in any situation. Anyone who wants to build upon one's emotional intelligence must take a good look at one's self.

There are several questions that people should ask themselves when they are thinking about their emotional intelligence. These can be used as often as needed while someone learns about how to build one's EQ skills:

1. Am I able to recognize my emotions when they happen?

2. What do I do when I am frustrated? Do I lose control?

These first two questions refer to how well a person can handle stress-filled situations. Those who know how to identify their emotions are already emotionally intelligent.

3. Am I good at listening to people?

4. What can I do when I am worried about things? How well am I able to calm myself and relax?

5. What can I do about organizing groups?

6. Is it easy for me to think about long-term goals?

These questions relate mainly to business. Having a plan for managing content is a necessity for the working environment.

7. What do I do when I am unhappy? Am I able to move on when something bad or upsetting happens?

8. How do I handle conflicts? Do I talk with people about what is happening or do I try to avoid conflicts?

A high EQ person is never upset for long. That person will do anything to see why he or she is upset and will work to correct issues or to keep conflicts from being a burden.

9. Do I enjoy what I do?

10. How well am I able to read other peoples' emotions?

11. Do I listen to other people when they speak? Do I hear their words and how they say things?

High EQ people are able to get along with those they meet. They also feel better about themselves because they are in situations where they are comfortable and know what they are doing to make themselves into better people.

Chapter 34 – Keeping a Journal

Journaling is a simple activity. People just write down what they are thinking about each day. However, journaling can be about more than that. When a person writes in a journal, that someone lists one's emotions and beliefs. Over time, they will start to notice if they are improving in some way. This also helps to figure out what can be done to improve life.

Journaling is not only helpful it is also a suitable activity for people aiming to build upon their emotional intelligence.

What Journaling Entails

A journal describes a person's daily thoughts. It can be about anything, but it is typically a person's observations and actions. Those who engage in journaling do it for many reasons. Some like to reflect on what they have done while others just want to be a little more creative. Regardless, journaling is a practice that will build one's EQ and make people feel better about themselves.

The journaling practice is simple and easy to follow:

1. At a certain point every day, write a new entry.

2. Include details on certain things, feelings, and actions that took place that day. The report can be as detailed as you want.

3. The things listed in the journal need to be as accurate and truthful as possible. It is best to keep from erasing things. Just be satisfied with whatever is in your mind at the time.

Journaling is an activity that a person will quickly start to look forward to each day.

Why Keep a Journal?

There are many positives that come with keeping a journal:

- A person will start to identify mistakes that were made during the day. This includes looking at what effects came out of certain actions and how they were harmful or beneficial.

- The mistakes that are noted can be analyzed based on what causes them to occur. As a result, a person will learn what to do to avoid those mistakes again.

- Problem-solving skills can be built through journaling. Just writing out one's thoughts can make a difference in figuring out what can be done in any situation.

- People who write journals become more self-aware. They notice that there are many things in their lives that are changing and making a real impact.

- Anything that someone has learned or discovered that day can be written in a journal. The new info will stay fresh as the content is documented from one's memory.

- People start to become mindful of themselves and others. There comes a point where the emotions and thoughts one has could have changed.

- The goals that people have become easier to recognize while writing a journal. Such goals can be about anything relating to relationships, money, jobs, friends, social activities, etc.

- Self-discipline becomes stronger through journaling. By identifying what is wrong, a person can take small steps to keep those issues from reoccurring.

- Journaling might help one's ability to speak to others. The changes occur when someone knows what words work best when conveying emotions and thoughts.

- Journaling makes anyone feel more confident. A person who journals feels as though he or she has done something positive or at least learned something new each day.

- Creativity is a key part of journaling. People who write journals start to find new ways to convey their emotions and thoughts to other people.

- People who write in their journals can heal their minds over time. When a person writes about their feelings or emotions, it becomes easier to want to move forward and have a better life.

The work that comes with journaling can be extensive at times, but it can be worthwhile when all the benefits are considered.

How to Use a Journal

To some, writing a journal is all about choosing a time and then writing about daily activities or thoughts and feelings. You can be as versatile with a journal as you want to be.

The steps for using a journal for building one's emotional intelligence are:

1. Decide on a platform or theme for the journal.

When developing emotional intelligence, it helps to create a theme for a journal based on one's emotions and how you felt throughout the day.

2. Find something to write with.

Although anyone can write a journal on a computer, it might be best to write an EQ journal on a physical notepad. Doing so allows a person to have extra time to think about what one wants to say and how well certain thoughts might happen.

3. Plan a time for when a journal entry will be written.

The best time to do this is at the end of the day when it is easy for to recall what happened during the day and the thoughts and emotions that happened. Keeping this time as consistent as possible allows a person to develop a positive habit of writing regularly.

4. Write the details on what happened in the day.

These details can be about practically anything - from the routine to the extraordinary, it helps to talk about anything that has gone on.

5. Explain the emotions being felt.

The emotions should relate to not only regular activities but also things that someone might have been surprised about. The writer should always be honest. It is not as though someone else is going to read your journal. Being honest allows for true emotions and thoughts.

6. Keep a sensible length for each journal entry.

A good idea is to keep the writing to a few minutes at the end of the day. Writing just one page could help. The writing should not be too elaborate or complex. It just needs to be good enough to where the writer knows what one wishes to convey.

7. Review how the emotions were felt.

After a few days of writing, it should be easy for a person to find trends in one's emotions. These include trends relating to what someone is doing and how happy that person might be or if there are worries. Any emotions that one might have felt should be written about.

8. Decide how to control those emotions.

Look at not only what causes certain emotions but also what triggers those emotions.

9. Over time, the journal should start to show real results based on what someone is doing with one's life.

All the journal pages will add up over time to create a full portrait of a person who wants to keep one's life under control. The journal creates a good plan for what can be done and how well life can be led based on the values and thoughts someone has.

Here's a good example of how journaling can work to boosting one's EQ. Janet might start writing her own journal each night in a physical notebook. She will write about what she did during the day and how she felt about it. She could also write about things that she observed, especially things that are out of the ordinary.

Janet will think more about what she feels she could have done to make it work better. Part of this includes thinking about what caused her emotions to be the way they were. She might also start to notice trends where she feels certain ways toward certain people.

As she reads through her journal, she starts to notice trends about what she is thinking and how she is handling her daily life. What she has written will give her ideas on how to control her emotions and protect herself.

This reviewing will cause Janet to become more self-aware. She will start to feel better about herself and realize that there are answers to the many concerns and issues she has. By deciding what she can do to change for the better, it becomes easier for her to move forward and to get something special out of her life.

Added Tips for Journaling

Several additional things should be noted when starting a journal. Here are some tips that people can follow for making their journals worthwhile:

1. Use a pen or pencil.

Although it is easy for people to type things on a computer, journaling for emotional intelligence works best when a traditional pen or pencil is used. Writing with a basic instrument allows a person to have time to think. This includes knowing how to get in touch with one's deepest thoughts and emotions.

2. Set a specific time for journaling each day.

Journaling at a certain time each day is a necessity for having more control. This includes establishing a habit that is worthwhile. The morning is often a popular time as it gives a person the ability to sort out one's thoughts before the day starts. But the evening can work too as it lets a person write about what has happened in the day and how they thought about it.

3. Write every day.

This aspect of journaling cannot be emphasized enough. People need to write every day if they want to get more out of their journaling efforts. Writing every day will develop into a regular habit that is positive and will have positive benefits.

4. Don't try to use a specific pattern while writing.

One mistake that people make when writing in a journal involves using a certain pattern. It is easier for people to grow their emotional intelligence when they write down their raw feelings. This includes working on what someone might be thinking without censoring.

Having an entry that includes one's raw thoughts helps to have a better idea of what emotions need to be controlled and how those feelings are formed. This keeps a person from unconsciously hiding some of the things that one is feeling without being aware of it.

5. Be patient when writing.

Patience allows someone to allow natural emotions to come out so they are documented without being altered, censored or covered up in any way.

6. Don't be afraid of the subject matter.

People are often reserved when they write in journals. The journal is designed to be private, so it should not be a problem for anyone to write about whatever is on one's mind.

Journaling is more than just a hobby for many people. It is also a practice that will make a difference in anyone's life. Managing the best possible journal for growing one's EQ can help to grow one's ability to identify emotions: how they occur when they occur, and why they occur.

Chapter 35 – The Value of Meditation

Meditation is a practice that has been used by people for centuries as a means of relaxing and being at ease with one's mind and body. It is a simple action that anyone can participate in to focus one's mind. The goal of meditation is to produce a mental state of inner calm.

What Makes Meditation Popular?

People participate in meditation for many intentions. Many of these purposes are linked to emotional intelligence.

1. All parts of the brain will synchronize with one another.

The brain will synchronize to improve its ability to pick up and learn things. This, in turn, improves upon how emotions might be interpreted and recognized. It is easier for a person's EQ to grow when the brain is fully functional. The added focus that comes with meditation also lets the brain become more creative. This added functionality within the brain keeps it active and ready for anything that may come about in life.

2. The brain's chemicals can function well when enough effort is put into meditation.

Much of what the brain does is based on the chemicals that go through the organ. Endorphins are vital for releasing positive feelings in the brain. Meditation helps to restore how those chemicals work. The production of cortisol is reduced. Cortisol is a compound that is produced in the brain when it suffers from a stress response and is unable to process thoughts and functions appropriately. Meditation reduces the pressure on the brain and allows it to relax. This allows the release of endorphins while also keeping cortisol production at a minimum.

Why Meditation Is Vital for EQ

People often do not think meditation is connected to EQ but it can help a person feel relaxed and confident.

1. Meditation gives a person time to be with one's thoughts.

Meditation helps organize thoughts so it becomes easier for them to understand and control.

2. It is easier for the brain to generate new connections while meditating.

For one's emotional intelligence to grow, the brain's plasticity needs to be supported. People have to look at what they are doing to manage their brain connections. By meditating, a person will be able to erase negative thoughts and think about the positive things in life. This produces a better result in the long run as the brain will respond better to its new functions, thus allowing for one's emotional intelligence to grow.

3. People can find reasons for why things are going a certain way when meditating.

With meditation, a person can take the time to think about what is happening in their life. This helps a person to grow emotionally without worrying about any problems surrounding them.

Emotional triggers can be identified while meditating. As a person thinks back to what has happened, they will start to notice that the worries or issues they have are irrational and based on false worries.

It is through meditation that a person can attain a better mindset and feel stronger about one's emotions and thoughts.

Steps for Meditating

It helps to look at where one is going when trying to meditate so it will be easier for the meditation process to work:

1. Choose a room in a house that is quiet. The area must be free of distractions and is comfortable.

2. Sit down in a comfortable position. Lying down will make it easier for someone to go to sleep. Part of meditation involves staying alert and aware of one's surroundings.

3. Think about a particular thing - a single event or even an item in a room. It should be something that can quickly be focused on without lots of distractions.

4. Think about what the item or event in question has to do with one's life. It could be anything that has happened, emotions that were felt, plans of some kind or thoughts of a peaceful place.

5. Focus on the item while recognizing what makes it important.

6. Be ready to question what is in one's mind while remaining calm.

There is no need to talk out loud, but it does help to talk to oneself internally. The key is to talk about the things relating to that item while being positive.

Is Sleep Fine Too?

It is clear that sleep is vital for the body. Everyone needs to get seven to nine hours of sleep each night so the brain can feel restored and ready for the next day. Getting enough sleep makes it easier for the brain to retain its plasticity, thus making it easier for one's emotional intelligence to expand and thrive.

That does not mean that sleep can work in the same way as meditation. When a person goes to sleep, it becomes hard for the brain to make connections between things that happened in the day. The brain will relax and will not focus on anything at all.

Meditation should be practiced when the brain is fully active and alert. Sleep allows the brain to shut down and restore itself and meditation lets the brain stay alert while creating connections between the things people see in their lives. Meditation gives the brain a purpose for understanding concepts.

Chapter 36 – Manage Deflections

It is often a challenge for people to think about what they want to get through arguments. People often do what they can to get ahead of others when arguing, but sometimes they notice that the things they are saying and doing are effective. Therefore, they try to make their arguments a little more personal. They do this by trying to deflect their opponent's arguments.

Deflections are often used by people when they are in disputes and want to find ways to change what people are feeling. This action is often confrontational and in some cases is used by people who do not have much of an argument and because they don't want to be fully responsible.

It is never pleasant to deal with deflections in one's life. People need to know what they can do to manage the deflections they have come across.

People who want to build their emotional intelligence should know that deflections can be reflected too. People should use the deflections that they are subjected to as ways to reflect upon who they are.

What Is a Deflection?

A deflection occurs when a person tries to change the direction of a discussion. For instance, Sally and Janet might be in a dispute over some topic in the workplace. They have an extended history and want to create a discussion over how to go forward.

Janet might have an opinion that is very different from Sally's. Because Sally's arguments are weak, she will try to deflect the question. She will change the topic and focus on something else. In this case, Sally might bring up a very different question to change the subject. She might even try to expose Janet's shortcomings.

Janet is trying to explain to Sally that she is wrong about something. Then Sally will deflect the issue and tell Janet that she is wrong, bringing up something very different.

The worst part about deflections is that they are generally immature and often keep a person from accepting responsibility. Instead of acknowledging that a person is wrong about something, they will instead try to force someone's hand.

Knowing how to manage deflections is critical to keeping one's life under control. It is through handling deflections that a person can use one's emotional intelligence to their benefit.

Understand Why People Deflect

There are many good reasons why people use deflection in an argument. Some people might deflect because they don't want to go too deep into the subject. People with strong EQs will be able to avoid deflections because they will fully understand what is causing those deflections to come about and become problematic.

1. A person is afraid of what might happen during an argument.

For instance, Sally might be deflecting what Janet is saying because Sally is afraid what might happen in a discussion. She might not be prepared to talk about something. Perhaps she feels a sense of worry about what is being discussed.

If Janet had a high EQ, she would talk about the issue with Sally. She might try to ask her why she is deflecting the issue. Janet could ask if Sally has some fear surrounding the topic in question.

By discussing the fears that Sally has, it becomes easier for her to feel comfortable with what is being discussed. She will not become worried about the things that are causing her to become fearful and worried.

2. Someone has irrational feelings that need to be discussed.

There is also the concern that someone has difficult feelings that are irrational and not based on facts. For instance, Sally might feel that she is right about something and that anyone who disagrees with her has some problems to work out. Sally might have some ideas of her own that she feels are correct even if they are not. Maybe those feelings are irrational. When a person feels threatened, they will try to deflect an argument.

The best thing for a high EQ person to do is to talk about those feelings. Talking it out helps to understand what is causing a person to feel this way. Delving deep into those emotions and how they are produced.

3. There's no other way for a person to make an argument.

Many people deflect issues because they have no other argument to work with. They think that by calling people names or making them feel bad is a way of changing someone's mind. In reality, it becomes obvious to notice that a deflection is taking place.

A high EQ person will be able to notice that someone is engaging in deflecting. This includes trying to keep a discussion from moving along smoothly.

4. Deflecting often feels good to people.

Sometimes a person just tries to enter into an argument to win. That someone will want to hear only the things that are in agreement with their mindset even if it is unusual or irrational.

5. Others just want to cope with the things happening in their lives.

People often get into real problems within their lives. Sometimes a person might be unhappy with what is happening in their life. This leads to that person deflecting a problem or issue. By using a deflection strategy, a person will chastise other people for what they have to say about someone. This move is designed to get someone to change their behaviors or actions even if this is difficult.

6. There is just an irrational hostility felt.

Hostility is often a one-way street in that a person does not like someone for whatever reason. Deflections are used against that someone to retaliate or to dominate them. In some cases, it is more about embarrassing someone or getting back at them over a perceived slight.

This is the most illogical type of deflection. It is also an irrational way of handling an argument. This will only hurt a relationship and make the people involved feel inadequate and upset with each other.

When building one's EQ, it will help to talk with a person about the issue at hand when deflections happen. A deflection is not always about anger or hostility. It is often about just trying to keep from getting into a dispute.

How to Manage Arguments That Entail Deflections

Deflection is not something that people often want to contend with because of how unusual or irrational a deflection is. Those who know what they can do to keep deflections in check will be more likely to succeed in having rational discussions.

1. Understand a person's emotions when deflecting.

Sometimes a person who deflects things might be in a rush to get over a dispute or debate. That person wants to get the topic out of the way fast before one's lack of preparation or knowledge becomes evident.

2. Determine the rationality of a person's deflection.

The deflection being used might not work as well as it could. For instance, a person who deflects might be proven wrong in some fashion and does not have an argument to present. There might also be times when a person's deflections are due to a personal vendetta or issue that someone has. Discovering how realistic or illogical a deflection is can make a difference when figuring out what someone is thinking or doing.

3. Don't try to forward a person's deflections or feed into them.

There are times when people might try to criticize someone's deflections. This is not always going to work. Instead of trying to manipulate the deflections, it is best to let the deflection run its course.

How to Avoid Deflections

People who are emotionally intelligent will know that they have to stop themselves from using deflection in an argument. There is always a temptation to deflect an argument when things are not going as planned. It is understandable because they often think that they need to change the focus of what is being discussed.

A person might be deflecting to keep from making positive changes to one's life. The reason might be that person is too afraid to acknowledge one's own shortcomings.

It is through deflections that a person might try to change opinions. This, in turn, makes it harder for a discussion to continue in the right direction.

There are a few things that can be done to improve one's EQ by managing deflections:

1. Start by thinking about the shame that comes with deflections.

People deflect things because they don't want to be responsible for what they are doing or saying. They deflect with the belief that by doing so, it becomes easier for them to go forward with any plans they have.

2. Be willing to address the sense of contempt that might come with a deflection.

Contempt is the most prominent feeling that occurs when it comes to deflections. The important point is to discover what is causing that contempt.

3. Instead of deflecting, reflect and look at an argument.

Sometimes an argument that does not go in one's direction will require a person to look into one's own mind. Part of this involves taking a look at why certain feelings might have come about in one's life.

When a person is criticized, there comes a need to reflect on it. Reflection is the opposite of deflection as it is about understanding why that criticism has come about.

Sometimes the criticism is understandable and logical. A person who reflects upon it will notice that there are things that can be done to change one's life for the better based on the criticism that someone has felt. In other cases, there is a need to look at whether or not the criticism is realistic or if there are problems with whatever is being discussed.

A high EQ person might catch oneself in the act of deflecting attention away from the subject being discussed. One needs to look into what is causing the deflection so it can be controlled and eventually stopped at some point.

Most deflections are illogical. They might even mask a person's inability to come up with a decent response to a question or issue. Avoiding deflections is critical, but being able to catch the deflection before it can move forward is a necessary skill.

Chapter 37 – The Threat of Multitasking on EQ (and How to Stop It)

Multitasking is often a challenge for people to think about what they are doing. A person might forget that there are different rules and standards associated with each task.

For instance, Jeff works for an advertising firm. He has many tasks involving creating advertising campaigns for multiple groups. Each of these businesses has its own standards for what needs to be done in their advertisements.

Jeff might try to work on each of these tasks at the same time. He will do this with the belief that by handling as many things as possible at once, he will be more productive. More importantly, he feels he will satisfy all of his clients.

Multitasking might not always be easy for Jeff. Maybe he has multiple deadlines to work with each of his clients. It will become easy for him to lose track of those deadlines, thus causing him to fail to do things right and on time.

Each of the clients Jeff is working for might have their own rules for what they want to be done. One company has a need to convey a message in a certain tone. Another wants a livelier approach with a more personal touch. By working on too many tasks at once, Jeff can mix up what he is doing and give the wrong results to the wrong client. This, in turn, results in serious problems where he has to correct everything he is doing and waste time, thus making it harder for him to keep his work intact. Worst of all, Jeff might end up losing some of his clients because he clearly did not keep each client separate from each other.

Jeff did not recognize how risky multi-tasking is, thus not helping his clients like he wanted to.

So, what does multitasking have to do with emotional intelligence? It occurs when people are afraid of falling behind in their work.

Several things can be considered when it comes to multi-tasking and emotional intelligence.

How Multi-Tasking Hurts the EQ

There are many good reasons why multi-tasking can be dangerous for one's EQ.

1. A person will not be self-aware of one's work when multitasking.

A person's EQ can be harmed while multitasking because they are too busy thinking about lots of things that have to be done at the same time. When a person is not self-aware, they start to focus too much on work and various random tasks. This becomes harder for people to handle at times because they aren't seeing the big picture.

2. Multi-tasking keeps people from being able to learn.

Those who have a high EQ are capable of learning things better than others because they have all the perspectives they need on a subject. It is easier for people to learn when they focus on just one thing at a time. Those who are busy trying to handle many things or ideas at once are likely to struggle.

Learning is all about maintaining a sense of focus. Those who can stay focused on what they want to do and keep on working toward their goals no matter what happens are likely to do more. When a person tries to work on too many things at once, they can create problems that they don't know how to solve

3. The emotions become harder for people to manage when they are multi-tasking.

It is harder for people to stay emotionally in control when they start multi-tasking. When a person does too many things, it becomes harder for that person's emotions to stay even. A person will not think about some of the issues that might come about when trying to do far too many things at once.

The added stress that comes with trying to multitask could be threatening due to all the work that comes with trying to finish things the right way.

4. People can alienate themselves from their coworkers when multitasking.

Alienation is a problem that can impact any working environment. This is an issue where a person will distance himself or herself from other people because they are too busy or fixated on things. They will be too preoccupied with whatever is happening in a certain environment and less on the other people.

Multitasking makes it more difficult for people to get along with other coworkers. When a person is too busy, they will stop thinking about the others in the environment that might keep them in check.

5. Those who multi-task might feel too confident in themselves. They begin to develop unrealistic expectations of what they can do and won't know that they are incorrect until it is too late.

Multitaskers often will find themselves in situations that they cannot finish. Initially, they feel that they can do many things, but they will become tired after a while.

Let's go back to Jeff. He feels that he can work on multiple projects and get them all handled throughout a day. Over time, he starts to feel overworked. He becomes fatigued to the point where he has to rest. Eventually, that fatigue causes him to break down, thus struggling to complete some of his tasks. As he is unable to finish his work, he starts to delay things. This leads to people being frustrated with what he is doing.

Multi-tasking is only going to make things hard to handle. All of these problems relating to multitasking are ones that can hurt a person's ability to get work done and to keep it organized. There is a way for people to keep the problems they come into from being harder to manage than necessary.

How to Avoid Multitasking

Multitasking will only do more to hurt anyone's emotional intelligence. That does not mean it has to be a problem that persists. Several things can be done to stop multitasking and to grow one's emotional intelligence:

1. Start by dividing tasks based on when they are needed to be completed.

The best thing to do is to have a schedule for when particular tasks need to be finished. Having a good schedule on hand is vital for keeping life organized while also seeing that one is not going to try and do lots of things at once.

2. Determine a priority for everything that has to happen.

Some tasks might be more important than others. One task might have to be finished sooner. Maybe another task has a larger value attached to it, like a project that pays more money or an academic task that influences one's grade.

Whatever task is more important at the moment should be the one that is worked on first. This ensures that a person recognizes the value of individual tasks and how certain ones might be more essential to complete than others

3. Keep to the schedule.

The most important thing is for the schedule to be followed as closely as possible. The schedule has to be organized so a person will stay focused on the task at hand and not be distracted by other tasks getting in the way.

4. Make time for breaks.

Everyone needs a break. A person cannot work for ten to twelve hours straight. That would be difficult to do, and those who do try to do so will only struggle with fatigue. A person should plan and schedule regular breaks.

Multitasking might sound like something valuable and helpful for one's life, but it is not always going to work the right way. The best way for a person to build one's EQ is to look at how multitasking can be avoided and how a sense of control can work better.

Can Multitasking Ever Be Acceptable?

Some people argue that multitasking is perfectly okay in many cases. The stereotypical image of the mother taking care of many things while managing her children is a fine example of this.

The problem with this is that anyone who is hurried and tries to do many things at once will likely fail. It takes an immense amount of experience and expertise to complete many things at once. Even then, a person might still fail at it.

Avoiding multitasking is best for one's life as it ensures that a person will not try to do too many things. The real goal is to stick with a plan for work that isn't hard to do and allows for a sense of control.

Chapter 38 – Emotional Intelligence During the Job Interview

A job interview can be a stressful affair for anyone. It is during the job interview that a first impression can be made. When a person makes a strong first impression, it becomes easier for them to be trusted and respected. The people who have the best job interviews are more likely to get the jobs that they want.

A person's ability to handle a job will often be based on the job interview. It is easy for people to not do well in the interview. Even the people who would be the best at their jobs would be rejected because they had poor interviews. Employers want workers who are confident. It is easy for an employer to miss a quality employee because of a poor job interview.

Employers often use many considerations when hiring people based on how they can handle their emotions. An employer will want to ensure that the people being hired are ones who are sure of themselves. They want people who are positive about themselves and know how to handle their emotions.

People who have been working on their EQ and can manage their EQ will know how to respond to a conversation and will be able to make a good impression during an interview.

Managing Criticism

There are often times when employers will criticize their candidates about certain things. An employer might ask about some kind of experience a person held in the past, for instance. The candidate should be willing to acknowledge the shortcomings that one has and what strengths they have. It is a very poor candidate who becomes defensive and confrontational in an interview.

Teamwork

Teamwork is critical for any workplace. It is through teamwork that jobs can be done, especially the ones that are complicated and require people with many skills.

High EQ people are willing to accept teamwork tasks and they know they can handle various roles. They are ready for the job but are always willing to think carefully about whatever might be done in a certain situation.

The most important point in an interview is to see how well a person can respond to questions involving teamwork. A high EQ person will respond by understanding the different roles while recognizing that one's actions will make an impact on everyone on the team.

A person should not try to take too much credit. A high EQ person will focus more on what everyone in the group has done. This includes knowing that it takes an entire group of people to resolve issues. More importantly, a person will have to avoid being judgmental or hard on others in any situation that comes about.

Talking About Failures

There are often times when employees talk about the things that they did wrong. A person with a high EQ must take some responsibility for what happened. This relates to accountability.

For instance, Jacob might be trying to get a job at a new accounting firm. He might explain that there was a problem at his old workplace where certain accounting reports were not filed properly. If Jacob had a high EQ, he would explain that he was responsible and that he knows what he might have done that caused certain issues to happen.

If Jacob's EQ was low, he would try to blame other people. He would skirt his way around what he has done and try to insist that he cannot be held responsible.

Small Talk In the Interview

Small talk in a job interview refers to some of the asides that might be part of the conversation.

Let's go back to Jacob. Jacob might be willing to engage in the small talk that the interviewer starts. Jacob has a high EQ and he shows he is not worried to get into a chat about something rather minor. He knows that it is perfectly fine for him to talk to the interviewer about anything that might be interesting.

If Jacob had a low EQ, he would try to steer away from the small talk. He might feel that the talk is something to be afraid of because he would not feel that he had anything to contribute.

Those who have a better EQ will not be worried about it. Small talk is just a natural part of any conversation. Engaging in small talk is an indication that they are willing to relax and feel at ease with whatever is being talked about.

An Interest In the Position

Every person in a job interview has to show some interest in the job they are applying for.

A person who shows a genuine interest and enthusiasm in a job will be more likely to be hired. That person will show that the monetary aspect of the job is only a small part of what makes that position interesting and worthwhile. A high EQ person always shows interest in the opportunity to be considered for a position. A low EQ person will show indifference and would not be certain about their skills or what is required for the job in question.

A Willingness to Concede

A high EQ person will have a willingness to concede things as needed. This includes accepting certain changes in a culture of the environment. Those changes are all planned based on what someone feels needs to be done and how new ideas and concepts can come about in the workplace.

Concessions are not things that all people like to think about. Those who have strong emotional control over their lives will know that they can keep working and doing things in their lives even if they cannot get what they want every single time.

A prospective employee who is not willing to concede things is not going to be trusted by an employer. It would be harder for that person to get a good job at this juncture.

The questions that may come about during a job interview can be daunting for anyone. The experiences that come along might be just as challenging to go through. Those who are capable of handling an interview well, are prepared, and know what to expect will succeed.

Chapter 39 – Emotional Intelligence When Speaking in Public

One of the greatest fears that many people have is speaking in public. As important as it can be to address a grouping of people, it can also be stressful.

It is very easy for low EQ people to struggle when speaking in public. Those who are emotionally intelligent will understand what they have to do to make it easier for them to get through a speech successfully.

Be Confident

It is through one's self-awareness that it becomes easy for a person to know what to say and be confident in one's abilities.

A person who needs to go out on stage to speak will have to have their speech well planned and should have practiced beforehand.

The key for EQ in this situation is to look at the feelings on has before getting on stage. Are there things to worry about? Look for the reasons for those worries and resolve them before speaking.

Being aware of one's emotions and focusing on being confident and smart about one's feelings is vital for success.

Managing Feelings

It is understandable why so many people become nervous before they speak in public. Whether it is a boardroom with six people or a larger auditorium with a couple hundred people, anyone can become nervous before speaking.

Emotionally intelligent people will know how to handle a speech beforehand and will be able to manage their feelings. Although being confident is important, it is also critical to be sure of your subject matter and to have practiced your speech beforehand.

- Look at the reason for feeling anxious or worried. Is the fear realistic?

- There are often feelings where a person is intimidated. What is causing that someone to feel this way? Sometimes a person who is intimidated is being pressured by some misconception. A high EQ person will look into the source and figure out if it is realistic or just a silly issue that can be cast aside.

- There must also be a way to feel energetic and ready to speak. A high EQ individual always looks at the things in a speech that will be intriguing and worthwhile to everyone.

- The intelligence that everyone has to work with must also be explored in detail. The audience should be probed based on what they are interested in. It becomes easier for a high EQ person to work when that someone plans a speech based on what they are interested in. Finding a common bond between the two sides is critical to one's success.

The best way to talk with people en masse is to have positive feelings and feel confident in one's ability.

Addressing the Main Fears

It is not every day that people are going to have to make a speech. There are some good reasons why people are afraid of speaking in public.

Even more importantly, a person can use one's EQ to counter those fears. There are a few things that can be done in this case.

1. What if people reject the speech?

A fear of rejection is common among speakers. A speaker will always be at risk of being rejected. The rejection can be shown by ridiculing what someone says, walking out early, not laughing at a joke, or not participating in a question period.

High EQ people know that rejection is not always about them or how the speech is delivered. Rather, it is about a person's own perceived biases and beliefs. A person who disagrees with a speech or whatever is being introduced will be more likely to shun a speech. Then again, the real question is why that person was there in the first place if it was clear that someone is not going to change one's mind about something.

2. What if something really bad and embarrassing happens in a speech?

Realism is a point that high EQ people use when speaking. The goal is to look at how realistic problems with a speech might be. There needs to be understanding of how someone might not fully understand whatever is being introduced at a time.

The odds are the fears one has are unfounded. Those fears are points that someone might not realize are irrational or nonsensical.

3. What if the questions being asked by the audience are difficult to answer?

People are often afraid of the questions that will be asked. They might think they would get difficult questions that are nonsensical or otherwise hard to answer.

The main root of this fear is that someone might be challenged while not knowing enough about what is being discussed. The best thing a high EQ person can do is find a way to say "I don't know." This could be an answer like "We don't have the answers to this, but we are hoping to find them in the future".

Show Interest

The most emotionally invested people in any speech are the ones who have the most interest in the subject of the speech. For instance, there might a speech about some scientific discovery that was found in the chemistry field. The average person has only a layman's knowledge of the field of chemistry. A person who knows all about chemistry will be more interested in it. Having the speaker be someone directly involved with that scientific discovery might even be better

The person speaking must have some interest in whatever is being discussed. A high EQ person will think about the background of the speech and have an understanding of what makes the speech important and valuable.

Reason for Emotion

Emotionally intelligent people understand that there are certain things that can be said in a speech and what should be avoided. Knowing what to say and what to leave out is vital for success.

There has to be a reason why certain emotions are happening in a discussion. A high EQ person will work with many strategies like the following:

- Understanding the key points that need to be addressed

- Deciding what to include versus what should be left out

- Noting what is relevant in a discussion versus what is irrelevant

- Finding examples that can be used in a discussion; these include points that help illustrate a point

- Choose the right language based on the audience

- Getting the audience involved; this might be asking questions that will intrigue the audience or even reaching out to specific people for input

The main point about speaking is that it requires knowing how to give information to people in a way that they can follow:

1. Information is produced.

2. Emotions are generated.

3. People become more intelligent when they understand a concept.

4. The speaker will address the audience and make everyone feel confident and comfortable with whatever was being discussed at the start.

Appealing to reason can work well if the reason is logical. People are always willing to listen if whatever someone is saying makes sense and is easy to follow. People prefer others who know what they are saying and are willing to share their ideas.

Managing a Sense of Focus

Although the speaker is very important, they are not as important as the subject matter or content. Of course, the audience is essential. The content being offered should be planned based on the audience that will listen to the speech. It is the audience that is going to decide if a speech is successful or not. The audience members are going to judge the content of the speech, not the speaker.

A high EQ person will know that it is the message that is important. Knowing how to create an interesting message without being complicated is a must.

There are a few things that can be done to emotionally prepare for a speech:

1. Be aware of what the audience wants to hear. Try to adjust the speech accordingly.

The emotions of the audience can vary but the speaker should plan a speech based on what the audience might have an interest in above all else. This includes knowing what the audience wants to hear in a speech and how the points being introduced are to be highlighted.

2. Find ways to help the audience.

A high EQ person will know that the audience might be interested in a speech but just needs that extra boost to make them interested. Part of what can be done to make a speech easy to handle entails talking to the audience about the basics that will be explored in a discussion. This includes looking at what it takes for a speech to move forward without being complicated.

A portion of the speech might be reserved for explaining the background of a certain situation. This includes talking about the terms that someone might not be familiar with or might want to learn a little more about.

3. Keep the speech personal.

Part of emotional intelligence involves understanding that the people who are going to attend a speech are aware of what they are getting into. They know that they will be hearing about some topic that might be of interest to them. A great idea for a high EQ person to use involves keeping a speech as personal and controlled as possible. This includes addressing many of the questions or issues that someone might hold regarding a particular topic.

It is by looking into the personal aspects of a speech that such an event can be successful.

4. Be willing to let everyone relax.

High EQ people know that when they talk to people, they want to let them feel at ease. They know that those people who are listening will have their own interests but might be confused about the topic of the speech. Allowing the people to relax at some point in the speech is always worthwhile. This could happen at the beginning or maybe in the middle.

To get people to relax can be as follows:

- Tell a story about the subject matter.

- Tell a good joke about the subject at hand. A little lightheartedness never hurt as it makes people more interested.

- Talk about a problem people might have and see how well that issue can be resolved based on the speech. Talking about how a problem will be addressed is vital for allowing a discussion to move forward and be interesting to the audience. More importantly, it gives the audience something that they can take with them after the speech is over.

Everyone will feel better about a speech once they see that there is something great to talk about. This includes everyone feeling comfortable about the topic.

5. Be kind to the audience.

A high EQ person is never going to berate the audience or criticize them. Rather, that person will look into why an audience feels a certain way and then tailor a speech to see if that person can either confirm beliefs or change them depending on what will come in the speech.

Emotional intelligence involves knowing that there is always a reason why people feel a certain way about a subject. There are always going to be cases where people will stick to their values and opinions no matter what happens, but there are also times when people are willing to be flexible.

What If Someone In the Audience Becomes Difficult?

There is always a chance that someone in the audience might be belligerent. Someone might call out the speaker and be critical of something and be very vocal. This could happen in any situation, although it is a point that often comes about when talking about more controversial or suggestive topics that are challenging.

Knowing how to handle the audience and keep it under control is essential. There are a few things that a person can do to managing a difficult audience member:

1. Always be calm.

It only takes a moment for the brain to become frustrated and agitated when an interruption happens as someone becomes hard to manage. There is a need to stay calm at this point so it is not difficult for a speaker to continue. More importantly, the speaker needs to be calm when offering a response to the issues or concerns that the person has expressed.

Panicking about the situation is not a good idea.

2. Look at what the audience member is feeling. What is causing that person to act this way?

The person who is interrupting might have some background that causes them to think differently. This could include having certain attitudes or beliefs that are different or opposed to what the speaker is talking about.

3. Determine what that person's emotions might be.

Listen to the tone of their voice or how that person's body is being projected. This gives an idea of how angry or hostile someone could be or if that person is willing to listen.

Be aware that sometimes a person who wants to interrupt will be cordial and kind about it. That person might simply want to make a quick correction about what they think is wrong. The situation should not be too intense but calm enough to keep a person from being frustrated and worried.

4. Be respectful when addressing that person.

It is fine to address a person who disagrees so long as it is done in a respectful and careful manner. This point should be used even when a person sounds upset. It may not mean that person is actually angry.

5. When offering a rebuttal, the point should be relevant to the speech while not chastising the objector.

A high EQ person will know that the objector has some reason for expressing disdain or disapproval of a subject. When a person works alongside that EQ issue, it becomes easier for someone to avoid problems like a heated argument.

The most important point in this situation is to avoid going too far in the discussion. Do not turn the situation into a back-and-forth affair. Getting into such a debate with someone can become harder for people to take one another seriously when there is a strong debate between both sides.

The main point of this chapter is that public speaking can be a challenge for anyone. Those who are ready to engage an audience in a fair and sensible manner will be likely to move forward and succeed. A great speech will be one that runs properly and anyone who is listening will appreciate what is being said and not get into any difficult confrontations.

Chapter 40 – Creating a Strong First Impression

The job interview or a speech to the public is just one part of creating a first impression. An emotionally intelligent person will do much more to create a better first impression that portrays a person who is confident and comfortable with their dealings in life.

People with high EQs are capable of managing their first impressions the right way because they know how to handle themselves. They are aware of their emotions and know how to keep them under control.

There are many things that a high EQ person should do when creating a better first impression. These behaviors allow someone to show that he or she knows what one's role in life is and that there's not going to be any problems with whatever it is that person wants to do.

1. Keep a good open posture.

High EQ people always keep themselves open to ideas. Sometimes the ideas they hear from other people may end up being better than the ideas they came up with themselves.

A person should keep one's hands on their sides while standing straight up. The hands should not be kept on the hips with the elbows pointing outward. That position shows a sign of aggressiveness and a desire to dominate. It could also show a sense of challenge.

2. Keep strong eye contact.

People need to establish eye contact with each other if they want to show that they care about one another. Eye contact ensures that a person is paying attention and is aware of the emotions another person in the conversation has.

3. Use a strong handshake.

The handshake is a good link that must be used before a conversation can take place. It is through a handshake that a person's interest can be gauged. The handshake should not be too strong. Anything too powerful might be a sign of aggression or dominance.

4. Never touch the face.

Anyone who touches their face might be interpreted as being bored, uncertain about things, reserved or otherwise dishonest. High EQ people will do what they can to show that they can be trusted, thus avoid touching their faces.

5. Be active when listening.

Refer back to the section on active listening in this guide for more details. This is a vital point of any conversation, but it is even more essential for a first impression. When someone actively listens to another person, it becomes easier for a conversation to move forward and to feel a little easier to manage and handle.

The first impression can quickly become one's last if not handled right. Anyone who wants to offer a good first impression must see what can be done to control the issue and to make it easier to follow without hassles.

Chapter 41 – Emotional Intelligence In a Romantic Relationship

Much of this guide has been about the use of emotional intelligence when getting along with others in a professional setting. Having a strong EQ is needed to advance in the workplace and society. But what about emotional intelligence and romance?

Romantic relationships are very different from business ones. While a healthy business relationship allows people to feel good about their professional efforts, a romantic relationship can be intense. It could involve companionship and a desire to be needed and wanted. Sometimes the partnership can develop into marriage, children, and so forth.

Emotional intelligence is vital for romance for many reasons:

- It allows people to recognize that their partners have their own feelings, attitudes, and concerns.

- It becomes easier for disputes in a relationship to be resolved or even avoided.

- A sense of importance will also come about as people start to notice what they can do to keep their minds at ease.

Having a great sense of emotional intelligence will allow any romantic relationship with a man or woman to stay strong. There are several aspects of EQ to use in this chapter with regards to managing a more intense relationship the right way.

1. Be ready to understand the difference between needing someone and wanting someone.

When a person needs another, they are clearly dependent on that other person. For instance, John and Jane have been dating each other for years. John might want Jane's companionship because she is a great person to be around. Jane might feel the same way as she knows that John is a person she can trust and confide in.

What if John and Jane needed each other? At that point, the two would realize that neither of them can live without the other. They will do everything they can at this point to be devoted to each other.

An emotionally smart person will know that there is a clear difference between want and need. It is more important to want someone in that a good relationship could persist for years. But if one person needed the other, the relationship could become difficult and possibly one-sided.

2. Emotionally smart people are always willing to address how bad they feel.

Being ready to acknowledge when someone did something wrong is always hard. No one wants to be wrong. Sometimes, it takes an acknowledgment of guilt and fault to move ahead.

An emotionally smart person is someone who knows that being defensive when something bad happens is only going to make things worse. When trying to manage one's life and attitude, there is a need for a person to be aware of how others feel when they are hurt.

3. Self-forgiveness is vital for a relationship.

There might be times when it is difficult for people to forgive one another. The transgressions that might happen in a relationship can be intense

It is vital for high EQ people to accept the things they are doing in their lives. This includes knowing that it might not be easy for them to change things, but they can at least put in a conscious effort to make themselves happy.

A high EQ person is not going to dwell upon the bad things in life for too long. When a person has the EQ one needs for life, it becomes easier for them to pay attention to what they want to do in a good relationship that one can trust in and support in the long term.

4. People in a romantic relationship must be responsible for their emotions.

A good relationship will develop between people who are willing to get in touch with each other and share their values and thoughts in a peaceful and confident manner. Those who are responsible and willing to acknowledge their emotions are more likely to thrive and become better people in their relationships.

A person will not blame someone else. Going back to John and Jane, John might say that he is frustrated and that his job is harder than he anticipated. John is not going to blame Jane for any of this. He knows that Jane has a life outside of his and that the two are simply trying to get along with one another without creating any problems.

The same can be said with Jane. She feels that her job is stressful too and that there are lots of difficult people in her workplace who are making her job difficult. At the same time, Jane knows that John's work is completely separate from her own. Her high EQ allows her to remain positive. The two have many problems in their lives and some unmet needs. Through their interactions with one another, it becomes easier for them to get along and feel good about what each other might be doing.

5. People in romantic relationships focus not only on what they feel but also what their romantic partner feels and needs.

Emotions are a two-way street in a romantic relationship. A high EQ person will acknowledge that there are positive things that can be said about one's life. They do not dwell on the negatives but find solutions that will accommodate and satisfy both partners in the relationship.

6. EQ should be used to decide how intimate a person wants to be.

It is through someone's intimacy that things can change in life. A person who is intimate and romantic will be more likely to be appreciated by their partner. A high EQ person will use their nonverbal skills to determine whether a person is open for intimacy. A person might show a lack of interest in being intimate if that person's arms are folded or if that person is trying to keep one's body away.

A high EQ person should review the lack of interest in intimacy and then figure out if there is a reason for it. They can ask their partner why they feel removed and start a conversation that is not combative or accusatory. More importantly, a person with a strong EQ will not risk forcing someone into sex or intimacy. A high EQ will want to let their partner feel comfortable about a situation.

7. Demands should not be imposed.

One way how people destroy their relationships is by trying to impose too many demands. These include demands that are not always easy for people to follow.

When a low EQ person will try to dictate and impose rules in a relationship for the partner to follow and the demands may not be reasonable or fair.

A high EQ person will be accepting of the ways their partner might live. For John and Jane, John will understand that Jane has her own interests. While he might like it when she wears certain outfits, he understands that Jane has her own ideas about what she wants to wear. It is not up to him to dictate to her

Quick Tips for Managing Romantic Relationships

Anyone who wants to keep a great romantic relationship healthy can use a few tips relating to EQ.

1. Always be appreciative. Resentful emotions do more to repel people than endear them.

2. There is no reason to debate an emotion. Disputing an emotion will only damage the relationship.

3. People should feel empathy for the other person in a relationship. They should not be defensive.

4. Do not assume that a partner is feeling a certain way. There is a chance that a person has a good reason for one's behavior. Sometimes a person might try to hide certain emotions without explaining them to anyone.

5. No one should ever use a partner's words against them. This attack becomes personal and shows feelings of hostility.

6. Allow a partner's feelings to have high priority. This is to show an interest in that person and a desire to express appreciation for whatever that someone might be doing or attaining in life.

Understanding Sexual Desires

It is no surprise that many people have sexual interests when it comes to relationships. Some people might want to enjoy sex because they really want to get deep into a relationship with someone. The problem with sexual desires is that sometimes a person might not be all that interested in sex. One's partner might not want to rush things.

This leads to the next point of emotional intelligence. Sex is only natural, but it is through one's emotional intelligence that it can make a difference.

There are three parts of the human experience that are vital for sex. A high EQ person should be capable of understanding all three of these points:

1. Love

First, there has to be a clear sense of love between the two people involved. The people who want to engage in sex should be cautious. They have to show that they appreciate each other. A high EQ person will analyze how the situation has grown and will see if the love that is coming from both sides is genuine.

2. Trust

There must also be a sense of trust in a relationship. The high EQ personality always thinks about how well a romantic partner is and looks at how honest they are. This includes reviewing one's body language to see if that person is physically open for touching. Looking into how often someone gets into one's personal space with proxemics in mind helps too.

The trust in a relationship should be high if people want to get into sexual affairs. It is through the added feelings of comfort and confidence that people will want to get into sexual relationships with each other.

3. A Need to Care

The two people must also have a sense of caring. This sensation can be identified based on how close two people are and how much they want to be near each other. When two people show that they care and they can easily read this feeling, it is easier for them to feel a desire to have sex.

There needs to be consent between the two parties. When a high EQ person identifies these three points listed above they will know that there is consent in a relationship that can make it really move forward. Of course, that person should still ask his or her partner about sex beforehand just to be safe.

What If One Person Is Overly Verbal or Emotional?

There are often times when a single person in a romantic relationship might be far too verbal or might take that person's feelings to extremes. For instance, a person might express one's feelings in a certain series of ways:

- A person might want to be loud and could start yelling or shouting.

- Someone could be overly angry and frustrated over even the slightest things. This causes a person to become verbal to where one would keep repeating the same things in a conversation.

- Someone could walk away from a discussion and not want to address whatever is happening in that chatter.

- It is easy for people to break down and start crying after a while.

It is at this point where a person is in the most need. These are not necessarily cases where someone is asking for attention or is being immature. Rather, they are moments when a person might really need assistance with getting something out of life.

A high EQ person will need to ask a person why that someone is feeling so emotional. There might be some issues in a romantic relationship that is keeping a person from feeling positive. There could also be cases where someone is too fixated on something negative. The key for a high EQ person to follow is to ask one's partner about the issue and to talk it through. The goal should be to find answers to whatever someone might be feeling and how to resolve the problems that have come along. Knowing how to get these issues under control without problems can be a vital point in life for anyone to follow.

Romance is beautiful and should never be discounted. It is critical to have a strong sense of emotions when looking to get more out of a relationship. Anyone who is emotionally strong and ready to handle any obstacle in life will be easier to trust and appreciate. It is through one's EQ that it becomes easier for a person to feel positive and comfortable with anything that might happen. There will be a need to keep one's emotions under control without being harsh on others.

Chapter 42 – Common Questions to Ask Oneself When Gauging One's Emotional Intelligence

The questions listed in this chapter are self-assessment points that help people understand what they are doing with their lives. Having a sense of understanding and comprehension about one's EQ is a must for having a better and more controlled life in any situation.

1. How well am I able to manage many priorities in life?

A person with a high EQ will know how to keep their priorities under control so they are not complicated or hard to work with. Those who accept too many tasks at a time will be confused easily with what they want to do. When a person tries to do too many things at once, that person becomes emotionally unsettled.

Those with high EQs will know how to organize their many tasks. They know that multitasking is dangerous and can be a threat to their emotional health.

2. How am I able to manage conflicts? Are there any conflicts I got into in the past, and what did I do to settle those issues?

Workplace conflicts can happen for a multitude of reasons – too many to list. Other conflicts may occur outside of the workplace and include relationship issues with a significant other or some relative. Whatever the conflicts might be, one should look at how conflicts were handled in the past. A high EQ person will know what to do to get beyond the problems and to keep them from being a threat or burden in life. Having control over one's emotions makes it easier to overcome any obstacles or hassles that might be a hindrance to a peaceful life.

3. How have I been able to manage challenges in life?

When encountering a challenge, one needs to keep emotions managed in order to think rationally and not make rash decisions. People with a high EQ are capable of knowing what they can do to overcome challenges and how they can resolve them before they become too severe.

4. Are there any points in my life that I feel I need to expand upon? What can I do with my life to make it better?

People with a high EQ understand what they can do to positively change their lives. It is important for people to look at how well their emotional states are managed. Anyone with a high EQ will find legitimate ways to resolve the problems that one has. This includes working to solve issues relating to the actions one is participating in.

5. What did I do when things that were going on around me went wrong?

A low EQ person will not have much control over what happens when life goes awry and nothing is going as planned. Someone like this might become emotionally unstable without being able to think about what to do to resolve the problems that have suddenly come about in life.

A high EQ person will treat the situation a little differently. That person will think more positively about what is happening. They will look for the silver linings in situations.

People who have strong EQs will know what to do when life does not go right. They will think reasonably and rationally about possible solutions.

6. What environment best suits my personality?

Everyone has an environment or situation that one truly shines in. A person might do well in a certain part of the office or performing certain tasks, for instance. Maybe someone is better at being romantic than others.

High EQ people know that they are strong and are not going to dwell on their faults or issues for long. They are willing to notice that there are many good things happening in their lives and that they want to focus on them.

7. When did my priorities in life change and what did I do to adjust?

This last question focuses on the things in one's life that might change and become different. When a person's priorities change, the things that they want to do in life will surely change. People must look at what they are doing with their lives to see how well they can adjust their attitudes and feelings toward whatever might be happening in their lives.

Conclusion

It is often difficult for people to determine where they are going in their lives if they don't have control of their emotions. It is through a person's emotions that someone can share what he or she is feeling or to establish a guide for how to behave and act in society. Knowing what it takes to develop strong emotions and to feel comfortable with them is a necessity for living. It is through this that people can feel better about their lives and ready to take on the world.

Emotional intelligence gives a person the ability to understanding how to coexist in harmony with others they encounter in their lives.

Those who have a high EQ can do more in life and grow as an individual. More importantly, that person will share their ideas with others. People will take those ideas seriously and will especially benefit if they are sensible.

When working to build one's emotional intelligence, it is necessary to look at everything being done in the process. This includes an analysis of:

- How well a person is aware of one's emotions

- How to keep emotions under control

- Knowing how to manage various social situations

- Reflecting on the issues that come about within one's emotions

- Realizing that many people have emotions of their own

- Knowing what causes people to develop the emotions they experience

Be sure to review this guide often to understand how emotions are involved in every situation and decision in life. Knowing how to manage one's emotions is a vital part of success in life and making the most of it.

People who work on their emotional intelligence levels just might find some things about themselves that they never knew. The exciting discoveries that come about by noticing how to handle emotions are truly intriguing.

Preview of

Mastering Psychology:
Discover the Science behind Motivation, Productivity and Success (Overcome Procrastination and Laziness)

Chapter 1 – Understanding Motivation and Productivity

When a person in a workplace has a certain job to do, they might feel encouraged to get on that task and act as quickly as possible. However, not all people in the workplace feel the same way. Some people have their own individual reasons why they might want to do a particular chore and others might simply feel a lack of a desire to do it. All of these people are different because they are all being impacted by the concept of motivation in various ways. Some people might feel motivated to get to work, but their sources of motivation will come from different things. Some might be motivated by the potential to make money or to get a promotion. Others might be motivated to work with the fear that they might lose their jobs if they fail to work hard enough. Many people in the same environment might feel a distinct lack of motivation. These include people who feel they are incapable or that the task has no purpose. Others might just feel a sense of malaise or discontent.

Competition might be used as a source of motivation. While many people are motivated to help others and to be friendly, others could be motivated by focusing on their own achievements and treat a situation as a race between themselves and other people.

Whatever the case may be, it is vital to understand how motivation works and what makes it an effective tool in the workplace. It is an intriguing and extensive science in its own right, but it can be easily understood when the many aspects of the concept are reviewed.

A Basic Concept

Motivation is one of the more intriguing points about psychology. Motivation refers to the reasoning behind why a person does any action. It is what causes a person to engage in certain actions and why that person might repeat a particular behavior. Motivation refers to how interested a person is in something and how that person might become committed to a certain action. This may also relate to a person's desire to attain a particular goal.

Those who are not motivated will accomplish nothing. They will not know how to take care of themselves or understand how to make changes in their lives. More importantly, people might have no real direction in life. It would become difficult for a person to do any action if they do not have the motivation to do it.

It is through motivation that people feel a strong desire to do new things or to move forward with what they want to do. Businesses could benefit from understanding how motivation is needed for anyone to do anything. They could use the secrets involved to discover what causes their workers to act in the ways that they do.

An Impact on the Entire Individual

Motivation is critical to understand because it does not just impact one part of an individual's life. It directly influences every aspect of an individual's life including their self-worth. A person who feels motivated will feel confident or thoughtful. A person will know that there is a purpose in life and that hard work has rewards. Someone might work toward making money, becoming healthy, finding love and happiness, and so forth. There are no limits as to what someone might do when they feel motivated.

What Does It Mean to Be Productive?

No matter what one does to find motivation, the end result is always to be productive. It is about productivity through not only getting more things done but also with meeting and maintaining the various requirements in life.

Productivity and motivation are linked to each other. When a person is motivated, that person is capable of completing more tasks and doing more in life. It is easier for tasks in the workplace to be completed so a business eventually becomes more successful and efficient. Meanwhile, all the requirements one has for falling in love, having a family, establishing good relationships with workers and neighbors will be met when one is productive. By being motivated, the productivity that one is capable of tapping into will be fully unlocked. The desire to keep working and to do more with an understanding of why work is valuable will make a true impact on one's life.

A Consistent Process

An intriguing part of motivation is that it does not only occur at one given time. A person has to continue to stay motivated and positive about life in order to succeed and thrive.

More things can be done when someone is confident and continues to be motivated. It is through motivation that people are able to change their lives and consider the things they can do to change themselves. It is vital to stay motivated and positive about life to stay forward-looking and in control of one's life. When a task is appealing and worthwhile, it becomes easier to feel confident and positive while wanting to go forward.

Motivation has to keep on working even when someone meets a certain goal. Although that person might have been motivated to move forward in life and to keep working hard, motivation is still required to go forward. It is vital to keep feeling the same way and to keep on working hard and encouraged to keep on working and do good things for one's life or business.

A Necessity for Health

Motivation and productivity are not only needed for thinking about what can be done in the future. It is also about protecting one's mental health. One of the greatest worries that people often have is to not know what to do in life or what one's purpose might be. Those who do not feel motivated are incapable of functioning well in society or taking care of themselves because they do not know what their priorities are. They cannot move forward to make their lives stronger and more efficient.

Everything that people do in their lives comes from some motives that they have. People who are heavily motivated and know what they want to do are often capable of being more productive and successful. A person who does not have a purpose or does not feel motivated will not have much to do and will not be able to discover ways to get the most out of life. It is through motivation that people are capable of staying focused and capable of doing the things they want to do with their lives.

Many people might not be motivated if they are unable to keep their lives organized or in control. Those who do not know what they want to do with their lives are often at risk of hurting themselves because they do not understand what they can do to make changes. Small problems due to a lack of motivation and organization will only become worse if they do not know how to take care of a situation.

An Indirect Point

One vital aspect of motivation involves how it can be observed. It is not something that people can observe directly. It can be assessed by observing the things that a person is doing in life and how productive that person is. You can observe motivation when you view how people change their lives. For instance, a person might not have been motivated to have a healthy diet in the past. However, motivation might be observed when that person starts to change their dietary routine. Although the reasons why that person is changing their behavior are not visible, they could have had a health scare or might be at risk of a serious health problem. The motivation will clearly be noticeable through the effort and work they are doing to try to change their situation in some way.

Motivation can be seen by the things that a person does at work or at school. A student who works hard in their studies and participates in various after-school programs might be motivated to do one's best. Perhaps that person could be motivated to just simply get a scholarship for college or even an internship in the future.

Goal-Oriented

Motivation and productivity are often associated with goals. That is, people will feel encouraged to work on something if they have goals to achieve. People might have a desire to work toward a goal, but through motivation, more work can be done and the goal to be achieved easier and sooner. The person who completed a certain goal will feel confident and will have the motivation needed to continue if the right goals are established.

The types of goals that people have are varied and diverse. The goals of the individual are not always the same goals as their supervisors'. The ideal situation is when the goals of both are the same and the jobs are completed correctly and on time. An example of this might be something that happens in the workplace. An employee might be motivated to keep on working hard in the hopes of getting a better position in the workplace through a promotion.

Every person will have their own special goals that motivate them. While one person in the workplace might be motivated to work to be given a promotion, another might be motivated to make a business grow or to become more productive. Another employee might just be focused simply on earning money.

The motivation is the psychological influence for a person to want to continue working and doing certain tasks.

Different from Other Concepts

Although motivation and productivity are tied together, there is a distinct attitude that can be noticed within the work a person completes.

Satisfaction
Satisfaction is a concept that focuses on how a person feels positive when certain things are done. Motivation is different from this in that motivation is what leads people toward satisfaction. That is, satisfaction is a vital goal but it can only be attained when a person is motivated.

A person might consider how satisfaction feels and how it can only be attained when certain actions take place. Motivation may help get that person to move toward a state of satisfaction. The key is for a person to realize that by working toward a certain goal or being encouraged to engage in certain actions, they will achieve the end goal of being satisfied and positive about one's work.

Those who do not feel motivated might be incapable of feeling satisfied. They do not fully understand what they should be doing and this keeps them from going forward and getting the most out of their work. When a sensible plan for work is established and a person knows what one wants, it is easier to attain satisfaction.

Naturally, the number of things that can be done in life will relate heavily to one's satisfaction. People often feel satisfied when they notice that they have done more and have been capable of completing more tasks and chores than they intended to do. People know that they have many things on their plates from tasks in their jobs to many points in their personal lives. When someone is motivated, that person's productivity levels increase and they are more likely to accomplish major tasks and eventually become satisfied with the work done.

Inspiration

Although motivation and inspiration may sound rather similar to one another, they are very different. Inspiration focuses on creating a new thought pattern. It entails how a person is going to want to do things in life and focuses more on changing certain attitudes.

A person might have a desire to do something. That is, the person is inspired to feel a need to engage in activities that are more intriguing. There might be an underlying factor that might cause someone to want to do things. However, it is through motivation that propels someone to take action. People have to be motivated to want to keep working and do things in their lives.

A person might be inspired to do something by another person in a workplace or maybe by a family member. The motivation that one has could come from an inspiration to be like someone else. One ideal example is if a person sees a number of slim models and would become inspired to lose weight to look more like one of those models. The motivation is the thought process for that person to actually change their behavior or take action.

Having a sense of inspiration might help a person to become motivated. The inspiration is not necessarily going to cause that person to actually be motivated in the first place. It takes extra effort to help a person learn how to stay inspired and ready to work and act. The inspiration in question has to be positive and reflective of the needs that someone has in life. By establishing a strong relationship with an inspiration, it becomes easier for a person to stay focused. When that inspiration is lost or a person begins to have second thoughts about it, it becomes difficult to stay motivated and focused.

Manipulation

Manipulation is often seen as a more difficult part of psychology that is a challenge. This happens when someone feels or is made to feel that they have to work in certain ways. A person might be manipulated so that he or she will want to engage in certain actions. Manipulation happens when someone uses a force of some kind without the subject's permission or knowledge. People who manipulate others will do what they can to make people do things they would not ordinarily do on their own. Even though the manipulator might have the best of intentions and wants people to be productive and active, this is not always going to be the right kind of action for people to engage in. It could be ethically wrong because it keeps people from being able to make their own decisions and to be inspired to stay productive.

Motivation is a gentle aspect of psychology. It is not forcing people to take certain actions. Rather, it encourages people to specific actions. The people who are motivated can choose their own methods for going forward and to do better things in their lives. This may cause people to be more productive because they will be motivated by things or ideas that they feel comfortable with. They are not at risk of being harmed or impacted by anything negative.

One point that will be discussed later in this guide is the art of incentive motivation. This relates to encouraging people to engage in certain actions by offering rewards. This is gentler than manipulation because it does not involve forcing someone into an action. It is rather about simply letting someone know that there is a good reward available for doing something.

The Overall Goal of Motivation

The main point about motivation is that it is all about finding a way to make a person feel satisfied with something. It is getting a person to feel as though his or her efforts in the workplace or in school among other places are worthwhile and that a person will reap some benefit. By allowing a person to feel motivated, it becomes easier for a business to thrive and move forward. People who are motivated are capable of doing extra in the workplace. They know that there is something on the other end for them when they are working on a project. It is vital for anyone in the workplace to be aware of their contribution and that it is appreciated.

This also helps a person experience a sense of purpose. It is often difficult for people to feel happy about their lives if they do not see a purpose for whatever it is they are doing. By establishing a purpose, it becomes easier for someone to stay motivated and to want to keep moving forward.

Those who are not motivated will not understand why they are working or realize the benefits of their work. The questions they have about why they are doing certain things and what they have to offer within the workplace will make it more difficult for a person to want to keep working as they do not see the reasons for working.

The overall point about motivation is that it is something that can be rather intriguing and unique. The many things that can happen when motivation and productivity are considered are all worth exploring.

Made in the USA
Middletown, DE
05 October 2018